WHAT'S IN A BENDERSKUM

some stuff I think about dotted
with scribbles minus colour

Rocky van de Benderskum

A benderskum

CONTENTS

ABOUT THIS BOOK

Why have I made this book?
ell it's not really the best question
hatever the reason is will be lost in time

Eventually it will all become clear
ven if that seems unlikely at first
verybody will understand
ntertainment initially
specially self entertainment
nding hopefully with yours too

Doing this is fun as well but I
oubt many people will buy it
on't think that will worry me though

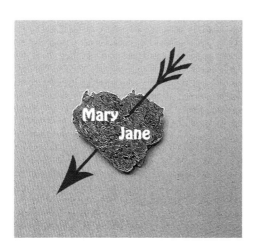

PAGES FILLED WITH BLAH, BLAH, BLAH

Try not to fall asleep

Gaps

Sometimes in life the hardest things to admit are gaps

Gaps in your thought processes
Gaps in your memories
Gaps in your brain
Gaps in ...

Just because I can't remember a date it isn't because I don't care

Just because I can't remember your name it's not because I don't care to

Not remembering if your birthday is on the 3rd or 4th or 5th or 14th

I'm sorry if this has ever caused you distress

It was never my intention
I may like you, I may not

It's not why I can't remember your name or date of birth

So if anyone ever asks about this

Show them this

Beware Of Buttons

from the original and genuine

Red Book of Nollidge

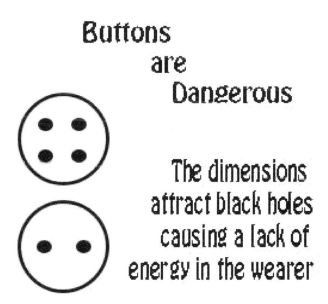

Buttons
are
Dangerous

The dimensions
attract black holes
causing a lack of
energy in the wearer

A word from Mileigh Mai Monk
Button Expert of
The Universal Fastener

Avoid buttons you can get sucked
into the black holes they contain

A Benderskum

Born in Malaysia, Skun up in a cave
Lived in a forest, must be depraved

Strangled my son to teach him respect
Got very skinny, but that's what you'd expect

My invisible friend is a weird guy called string
My life mantra is nonsense if that is a thing

When they gave me leukaemia to make me back down
That didn't work you can't make me frown

I think that two heads are better than one
But a bone marrow transplant was not so much fun

I don't give a toss if you like me or not
As long as my world still supplies me with pot

I'm just a benderskum and that's all that I'll be
Totally impervious you can't get to me

To keep up with my thought patterns you'll have to think so
much faster
Don't Pass Audit Prg Uber Liebe René's Caine Master Master

#thefake

Austerity

We don't have to live with right wing austerity
And whether or not you like my poetry
We don't have to follow the fat billionaires you need to know this
before it's too late
There is a way and really quite simple to put ample on every-
body's plate
To be a billionaire you must have something missing And don't be
mistaken it's not rich people I'm dissing
I admire quite openly folks, who've made fortunes from their
work
Though I'll never have such luxury I'm not the sort to shirk
I've never wanted riches just enough to live with ease
To leave me free to scribble and to pay my worldly fees But back
to that austerity a very unnecessary blight
On everyone who isn't rich and it isn't fucking right
It was invented by those in power just like the great depression
Something else that shouldn't have started another unnecessary
transgression
Though people are dying on our streets most people just walk by
So any hope of moral decency is merely pie in the sky
The far right are rising again has history taught us nothing?
Just like the rise of the Nazis this lot are really not bluffing
Hospital beds aren't empty they have simply disappeared
As our world is changing into something wrong a place to really
be feared
The climate is changing and getting real bad though many seem
not to have noticed
Believing instead the lies they are fed by the people whose coffers
are bloated
These are worrying times for the sick and disabled and children
and doctors and nurses
If I named all the people who it's worrying for I'd need many,
many, many more verses

But even the dragon like billionaires will eventually end up in hearses

You are born, go to school then it's soon time to work and you'll do this until you are dead

Well at least if retirement age gets much later and I'm quite sure that's something they've said

They say they've created a lot of new jobs some people have two jobs or more

But with minimum wage and zero hours contracts those poor folks will always be poor

I've got a confession that my facial expression

Hides behind it some pent up aggression

But it isn't just me there's a rising tide and it's spreading across the globe

For me it started deep down inside but it's now in my frontal lobe

We have to do something or what kind of world will be left to pass on to our young

As I said just before there is change in the air and I hope that it's truly begun

Cuts to social services and hospitals and schools

The fire brigade, police and more they really think we're fools

Although perhaps they could be right as the masses seem to follow

But I don't believe their rhetoric it's too bitter a pill to swallow

So what can we do to open your eyes?

Because everything they say is clearly lies

Thinly veiled deceit almost without a disguise

Are you really blind to the fact it's us that they despise It saddens me when I hear of the fact

Many species are extinct so there's no going back

Sixty percent of the Earth's animal population

Have gone since the seventies is no exaggeration

The seas are rising and they are full of plastic

We need to do something and something quite drastic If you really can't see it then maybe you're blind

Or totally stupid and that's me being kind

Cantheism What It Means To Me

Wow this religion, or more aptly spirituality thing is a minefield of misinformation and misleading links.

However I have concluded from this and my previous research on this very subject that it is an acceptable route to follow.

Having read more on pantheists and pantheism, it is obvious that I as I've always suspected I am 100% a Pantheist or more correctly for me personally a Cantheist, because of my belief that we as Homo sapiens co-evolved with and due to Cannabis.

> '*We must stop confusing religion and spirituality, Religion is a set of rules, regulations and rituals created by humans, which was supposed to help people grow spiritually. Due to human imperfection religion has become corrupt, political, divisive and a tool for power struggle'.*

Haile Selassie I

Definition Of A Pantheist;

Pantheists revere nature and the universe
Pantheists believe that God is Existence and Reality is identical with Divinity, therefore suggesting that the Universe is free of pre-determined destinies, while all the components that make the universe whole are determined by their interconnectedness to one another.

We respect and care about the rights of all humans and other living beings
We celebrate our lives and our bodies
We feel blessed to be a part of this beautiful earth it is a joy and a privilege
We have strong ties to our spiritual selves whilst maintaining a healthy respect for reason evidence and the scientific method to bring us understanding of nature and the wider Universe
We promote religious tolerance, freedom of religion and complete separation of state and religion, without the necessity to believe in supernatural realms, afterlives, beings or forces

Cantheist = Pantheist + Cannabis

Cantheists follow these same moral codes with the inclusion of Cannabis as a sacrament to better the lives of ourselves, our fellow human beings, and our world and in consequence our universe.

How that can lead into our predicament with Cannabis is one of the reasons I have set up a Cantheist Church, which doesn't necessarily mean needing a building for people to go and worship at.
A church is (at least) in Britain considered to be one of three things, a building, a concept or a group of people with the same belief.

Therein lays both the problem and the solution if we can all agree that this is our belief.
My core tenet of beliefs are;
I believe that humanity co-evolved with cannabis
I believe that Cannabis can alleviate a myriad of ailments and symptoms
I further believe some of the modern disorders are as a direct result of prohibition and the denial of my legal possession and subsequent usage of Cannabis.

This is furthered by my belief that many of the problems encountered on our world can be alleviated by the use of cannabis.

Further to my personal beliefs as stated above is my knowledge that some of my beliefs are also scientific facts.
There are known factors present in our everyday lives that further these beliefs
Insomuch as the environment is suffering, forests have been decimated and are needed as part of the lungs of the planet; it is unsustainable to continue, whereas Cannabis could be used in industries such as the paper, textiles and building industries to name but a few.

We have become addicted as a species to fossil fuels, oil, gas and coal, to the point that these are being depleted at an alarming rate and companies are looking at new and decidedly risky ways of obtaining more, at least in regards to our environment, including; Tar pit oil and chemical Fracking. The oil based industry being the worst is very short lived when you realise Petroleum became a major industry following the oil discovery at Oil Creek Pennsylvania in 1859, which is just a short 160 years ago, not very long in the greater scheme of things.
We know that everything made from Hydrocarbons could also be made from Carbohydrates but unlike for instance oil based plastics that only become microscopic and end up in the food chain, plastics made from plant materials are completely degradable.
Cloth made from Cannabis Hemp is a far superior product to cotton in so many ways; it grows without the need for vast amounts of (often oil based) chemicals in the form of Herbicides and pesticides and requires far less water. The material obtained after production is Thermodynamic, meaning it is warm in winter and cool in summer, it is fire retardant, water resistant and it doesn't become mildew if left damp unlike cotton.
Its seed is renowned for its nutritional content and is often used as a cereal and because of its ability to grow in so many different and often hostile to other food crops it could go a long way to end

starvation in countries affected by droughts etc.

Building materials produced from cannabis hemp due to the manufacturing processes involved sequester carbon from the atmosphere and become stronger with age as the carbon is absorbed into them.

As a Cantheist however I still don't believe in a monocrop of Cannabis/Hemp diversity is part of what makes life so enriching

Sixth Mass Extinction

There are holes in the sky where radiation gets in
But these holes are huge and will burn your skin
With a planet that's dying its long time for change
Or just try to ignore me and think that I'm strange
Moan about delays caused by planet protectors
And soon our world will be just full of spectres
I hope the word change will enter your head
For nothing can live on a world that is dead
You may do your recycling and think it's enough
But the world is a candle about to be snuffed
It's not actually too late there's still stuff we can do
But that includes everyone, you, you and you
We really need an end to the corporate greed
And stop keep on buying all that shit you don't need
When the air is polluted and the water is too
The only animals will soon all live in a zoo
Species are dying not just names on a list
Doesn't that make you shake your fist?

In the sixties they told us this was to come
But they were ignored so nothing was done
There are still people saying that it's just not the truth
While ignoring the facts and blind to the proof
When the government forms a department of death
Remember my words as we take our last breath

Save Ya Machine

Elections, Selections, Deflections

What ever pretty colour your party's rosette is,
I hope that you soon realise they all just take the piss
They aren't there for you and certainly not for me
They're only there to stay at the top of the political tree
You may feel this all seems simply quite abrupt
But then most politicians are simply quite corrupt
A leading politician decided to cross the road
Then claimed eighty quid expenses the thieving fucking toad
I admit that that's a joke of course because I'm not a liar
Eighty quid was just a start the claim would be much higher

A day or so it seems in the working life of a lord
Is to fall asleep on a leather seat the result of becoming bored
A day in the life of a common for surely that's what they are
Despite the fancy houses and the chauffer driven cars
Is meant to be what they promised when they stood in a general
election
But this is something hard to miss they are masters of deflection
They all have their own agendas and continue them when they
are able
While the promises they made to get your vote aren't even under
the table

So this is a reason anarchy is superior to the system we have at
present
I'm not even distantly roya. No but I'm still not a fucking peasant
I believe in the people's autonomy
not this crippled lop-sided economy

There once a great depression that wasn't so great I'm sure
An era when nobody had any work that ended up in a war
But that's just manipulation or maybe horses for courses
The workers and the factories were there and the natural re-

sources
So if you think my hats made of tin and all this stuff is just in my
head
Do the maths, look at the facts and carefully think about what I
just said
There was once a great depression it ended in a war
But the infrastructure to facilitate it was already there before

What ever pretty colour your party's rosette is,
Now have you figured out they all just take the piss
Homelessness. the poor or people who just aren't healthy
Not really on the agenda cos that won't keep them wealthy

All of my life I've watched our world get sold from under our feet
The owners now the oligarchs and political elite
Digging it up knocking it down to overload a purse
Destroying what once was beautiful nothing could be worse
We live in an autocracy although they call it a democracy
But everyone knows it's a big fat lie and maybe even hypocrisy

So instead of keep on asking for things that are already yours
Demand the end of this status quo and to change their fucking
laws
Or do your things in spite of them either will get you my applause

So rouse a politician, wake it from it's sleep
Say it's time to get a job and leave the leather seat

Very Late At Night

There is no proper answer and if I can't get a proper answer I'm quite likely to;
Very late at night when everyone is asleep, and just to make sure they are I'll send out my fleet of chloroform spray drones to dust the area.

Very late at night when everyone is asleep, and they will all be asleep because of the effect of the aforementioned chloroform spray drones.

Anyway, very late at night, have I already said that? Oh yeah, just checked, I have. So, very late at night when everyone is asleep, did I mention the chloroform spray drones, hold on I'll just a roll back up to make sure......
Yep! Ok, very late at night, fuck what was I saying?
Der, Der, Der, Der, ok got it.

Oh by the the way I wasn't calling anyone a Der it's just how I think so I thought I'd write down what I thunk.
Ok now I've got it, very late at night when everyone is asleep

Der Der Der Der...Der Spiegel autofuckingchanger

Der Spiegel that's a German newspaper ha ha ha
Where was again hold scroll back again now this is getting tiresome
Der Der Der Der Der Der. Ok, very late at night when everyone is asleep and it's really dark I will get into my teleportation device, well when I say get in, it's not quite a simple as that. What I actually mean is after stepping into my Shrinkage chamber and then simply reduce in stature to about the size of a one euro cent piece, or coin if you prefer but that's just semantics and whatever philosophical value you put on the actual word used. Damn I've forgotten where I was... Hold on
Der Der Der Der

So at this point I'm titchy you know like slightly over a centimetre tall, then easily walk I to the aforementioned teleportation device, ah did I mention the dead r...hang on
Der Der Der Der

I might be getting slow in me old age
Ok I'm in the teleportation device with and this is really important
With a dead rat that I just happened to have in my fridge, well when I say fridge I actually mean the cold room in my vast mansion in Muldovia. Anyway that's not important, not the rat , I mean the mansion and cold room, etc. Well it is actually important for the...Der Der Der Der Der Der Der Der Der Der
Look forget all that just know that I'm in the teleportation device with a dead rat in a celophane bag, note I'm not using plastic cos I don't like it
Damn there was a point to all this but what it was I simply can't remember
Apart from the fact that I have just given you something that I don't share with everyone
And I'm not talking about the dead rat that I put under your floorboards the other week oops! Forget I said that
No I've given you something quite valuable, well at least to me

What Climate Change Is That?

Ignore the debate
Our heads on your plate
You know it won't wait
Because then it's too late
If the temperatures rising why does it feel colder?
Questions like that only make you feel bolder
Hide all of the truth in one of your folders
So at least you'll be popular with the major stockholders
Of misdirection you are obviously masters
Blatantly ignoring all the natural disasters
When the news is all faked by your friendly broadcasters
The efforts you make are like sticking plasters
97% of actual climate experts totally agree
And their expert knowledge is good enough for me
That global warming is happening and it's definitely human-caused
Did you take all that in or is your brain still on pause
There really isn't time to waste we must do something now
Or carry on as always with the usual disavow
Venice council voted down any possible climate change action
Just after that it flooded and it felt like a chain reaction
Almost as if this was Karma but it gives me no satisfaction
Did it become major news here? No! There were too many other distractions
Last year we had the beast from the east, and in summer it was too fucking hot
You must have all noticed the seasons have totally gone to pot
This year it flooded and it's bound to get much worse
But they'll carry on lying as usual, copy chapter and verse
Minimization, Omission, Restructuring, are just three of the ways that they lie
Catching them out doesn't work either as then it's just flat out deny

So because of these things we can't leave it to them they simply aren't to be trusted

The way they behave as if nothing is wrong we ought to be fucking disgusted

But don't listen to me I know nothing you see then pretty soon we're gonna blow it

And by then it's too late to fix our mistakes and it's over before you know it

God

As I write this it's Sunday and if you get offended by my ramblings because you are a Christian oh well, shit happens.

First of all this is a bit (actually very, very) long I will forgive you if you skip reading it. I'm only writing it after being asked for stuff like this and it is just a taste of my life as I've been asked to write about which I may or may not publish one day.

I'm a Cantheist as such have similar spiritual mindfulness as some sects of many modern religions. Having said that I don't believe in a God figure or a group of suchlike.

First if I were a Pantheist I would believe that God and the universe are one and the same and in the interconnectedness of everything. However as a Cantheist I further believe that a vital part of that interconnectedness especially in vertebrates is our Endocannabinoid System discovered a mere 26 years ago, but every vertebrate has one, I'll post my picture of it at the end if anyone reading this doesn't know what that is. I believe that through the use of Cannabis my body attains homeostasis and my spirit or energy if only to avoid it sounding like hippy shit become balanced.

In my life I have done many things some were good things some were not; in amongst all that I believe I have atoned for any wrongs and am rewarded for good stuff, which is as it should be (moral homeostasis).

Cannabis helps me smile through the physical pains in my body undoubtedly caused by misuse, I did and still do have fun though, nowadays my body is my temple, I know it, I feel every part, likewise my brain is my library, but so much more my moral compass is quite diverse and very accepting of diversity, in fact it grows with diversity.

I love to learn on an equal scale as I love to teach, I believe that every person has the capability to achieve whatever they truly want to, there is no such thing as failure, it is merely a learning experience. I believe in mutual respect for one another's choices, but further to this I respect and cherish this wonderful place that we live in and its abundance which is unfortunately being systematically ruined by greed.

Our planet is an amazing place full of wonder if you look deeper than the surface you start to understand how everything connects and how similar things are yet so different

If you learn for instance how a plant takes up nutrients and water from the earth through a system of root cells and trap doors that only work one way forcing the same through narrow apertures causing it to increase in pressure thereby aiding its upward journey.

Then because hydrogen atoms have a positive charge and oxygen a negative you may know that unlike poles attract like poles repel in nature as in science, the atoms of the water attract each other on their upward struggle.

Photosynthesis causes a vacuum in the leaves further aiding this journey, how could you not be amazed at these different processes, chemicals, magnets, energy, vacuums and so on, inside a plant.

Anyway I'm rambling I started to talk about God well as I said that isn't really a thing for me. I stopped believing in God when I was about 7 years old.

I was quite a naughty 7 year old and for some reason one morning I was very late for school, this was in 1965 so there was no 4 wheel drive 'Chelsea Pushchairs' to take me, in fact not even an adult but that's how it was back then.

When I arrived everyone was at assembly so I just went to the classroom. I figured if I'm late at assembly it's a bigger deal than if I'm just late. I went in to the classroom, mooched about for a bit.

It was a Monday so when I opened the teachers drawer there was a tray containing everyone's dinner money and a book with dinner monies written on it mostly half crowns which was 2/6, two shillings and sixpence or for those who don't remember pre decimalisation, 12 and a half pence, for a whole weeks dinners so 6d a day.

My first and only thought was 'Treasure'. I pocketed the lot and went back out of school to a sweetshop nearby spent it all. Went back to school my class were still at assembly so I put all my booty in my desk, then bored went back outside waiting for my class to arrive.

We all went in the teacher took the register which I thought meant it wasn't noticed I'd been late, I was wrong it had been.

She then discovered the theft of the dinner monies told the prefects to watch us while she got the headmaster. They returned and searched the desk asked if anyone knew, anything then he left and I guess got the police. Later that morning I had just started to chew a fruit salad chew, when one of my classmates grassed me up for eating a sweet. That moment I knew I was doomed. The grass then said I'd got a desk full of sweets, which to be fair was true, I was only 7 and the enormity of my situation was just starting to dawn in my head, crikey I'm dead I thought.

They phoned my Father who was at work in town at the post office, he arrived steam coming out of his ears, not that I saw him arrive it was what I imagined, my dad by the way was big as in a giant not fat over 6 foot.

I went into the room there he was looking really pissed off, also a police sergeant, the headmaster and a vicar sort of person. My school was a strict Church of England place attached to Canterbury Cathedral. I believed in God because I mostly believed stuff adults told me and all that stuff was properly drummed into me. This was scary stuff; I wasn't bothered about any of them except my Dad, who I feared.

The headmaster asked where the sweets had come from as there was at least two pounds worth maybe three and at 4 a penny for many of them a huge bagful.

I said I found a bag of coins on my way to school and spent it all on sweets. Of course nobody believed me, but I stuck to my story. Then came the scariest bit of all I was told I had to pray to God for forgiveness for what I had done, I guess a confession.

The vicar bloke told me to kneel close my eyes put my hands together and tell God what I'd done and ask forgiveness.

So, I knelt and pretended to pray then said Amen, opened my eyes and said I've done it, hoping that would be enough.

The vicar said God was too busy to listen to thought prayers and it would have to be out loud. Now, bear in mind I was seven and believed in God, so also believed when he added if I lied to God he would strike me down with a thunderbolt.

Now although I believed it to be true and that terrified me it wasn't anything compared to the reality of my Dads face staring down at me with a look of extreme anger.

Once again I closed my eyes then said;

Dear Lord, forgive me for finding money, not handing it in then greedily going to the shops to buy sweets and not sharing them. Amen.

With my eyes still shut I waited to be struck by lightning it didn't happen and I knew at that moment I'd been lied to, I immediately stopped believing in God from that moment.

I was in a ton of trouble but never admitted to theft, no doubt my punishments for other naughty things I did were more severe for a while but nothing compared to what would have happened had I admitted the truth.

Queen Victoria is very unlikely to have approved of my behaviour but she was long gone, she would have I'm in no doubt not smoked spliffs either but she did like most people in her day use cannabis as a regular form of medication

Brockwell Park Brixton circa 2000

Mary Jane My Very First Love

I met Mary Jane for the very first more than forty years ago
An angry young man with a violent streak but she changed me after one blow
She appeared as a spliff in a bar in Quebec
From our very first kiss my anger she'd check
And over the years we have grown closer yet
But from those early days I wouldn't have bet
That I'd start my campaigning back when I was still strong
And still be at it now so what has gone wrong
We had cannabis marches right throughout the city
The reason it has changed is more than just a pity
The government decided to make it class C
Then as we backed off back up to class B
They always do something when the movement is growing
So you need to watch closely and then you'll be in the knowing
Their most powerful weapon needs little improvement
Constant division always weakens the movement
Some of the things argued over seem coincidental
That we argue over words is not accidental
But deliberately placed and probably governmental
Clever psychology but not transcendental
An article in a newspaper or on social media
But never an announcement they are way, way seedier
Keep on arguing over words or what we want it for
That does us damage and we'll never win this war
These things that divide us are deliberate deflectors
And not really helping our cannabinoid receptors
So what is the answer, what can we do?
And this is to everyone you, you and you
It really doesn't matter if you like me or not
I might lose some sleep but it won't be a lot
Don't keep losing sight of our ultimate aim
Our freedom to use cannabis without any blame

No comebacks from society including the law
Legalise, Decriminalise, licences and more
It's all totally unnecessary and really a bore
They lie through their teeth to keep their monopoly
They changed the law but did it so sloppily
Leaving no one with access but not accidental
They may be crazy but they're certainly not mental
If they changed all the laws and gave us autonomy
It would mess up their not so secret cannabis economy
They are very much aware of what happens abroad
And when we all squabble I bet they applaud
So division is a much bigger enemy than them
So it needs lots of pruning from the top of the stem
I hope that I've maybe planted a seed
Prohibition just stems from corporate greed
If we end our division it'll take away their power
That seed could then grow into beautiful flower
Recreational, Nutritional, industrial, medicinal, Sacramental
I don't mind why you use it I'm not that judgemental
I'd never question your reason to use
That's decision is entirely yours to choose
So try not to judge others and don't trip over a word
Or remain in division but that is absurd
So Canna Warriors please continue to fight
To get us back we know is our right
To use this great plant however we want
Make them retract and end this détente

Empty Page

Dit
bit
is
opzettelijk
leeg

Raindogs

Flavour

I sometimes when ordering my groceries go off on a complete tangent to food shopping. Today was one of those occasions.

Why is that? Well i after all the poison and stuff I've had pumped into me through three tubes i my chest, a couple of years ago, lol but there I go again, I mean tangents.

Der Der Der Der ah yeah, because of all that. The poison I mean, I taste far less than I would prefer, that section of the sentence looks like and sounded when I read it back like gibberish... I like that word it means a lot to me, gibberish, gibberish, gibberish, I first typed it with a capital G but it just doesn't look right. gibberish I mean not;

Don't Pass Audit Prg Uber liebe René's Caine Master Master

Because of course that is gibberish But what was I talking a bout agin Der Der Der Der, long thought that one but shopping, which I must also finish and actually order, at some stage in the near future before the page closes again for a third time oops.

If you read this far it was a while ago dunno, time is irrelevant here its light and has been since earlier and at some stage it'll get dark and I'll put the light on.

So in conclusion my shopping which I could have concluded several and hours ago was recently concluded. Oh and I obviously like the word concluded, you have guessed. I used to use Kelpermare it's a seaweed based liquid seasoning and very tasty, but I can't have seaweed, too much iodine with hyperthyroidism. I don't really want to use Nestle products, because they are cunts, End Of.

So that leaves salt luckily I like salt but even that has Iodine especially the pink healthy Himalayan stuff, I don't know if it's actually healthy or not I'm just a benderskum and a bit backward on some stuff, probably because to me at least they don't matter, either I like it or not, healthy or not, provided the contents aren't made of death   I don't care.

So whats it all about?

MSG Monosodiumglutamate E621 >>>THE DEVIL<<<

It turns out the tests they did were MSG was injected into rats, injected! Not eaten by rats, because of course that's exactly how humans have always got MSG in side us, I know you're all thinking I Fucking Don't.

Well maybe not all, some are probably thinking what the fuck is he talking about
 Me included.

But it gets worse the dose was a cow sized dose, you know dose makes it sound wrong but horse , not cow.

I quickly back read and noticed. You know give me an Elephant sized dose of Der Der Der Der I dunno er... this mythical medicinal cannabis I keep hearing about the different to the evil cannabis that makes grown men turn into bats, not that fucker.

Although now I come to think of it, er... yeah that one too it sounds proper.

So I ordered some stuff not made by cunts or from death with MSG, that I can presumably sprinkle on my food or in my cooking to make me like the taste again. This is my reasoning if it is as it's called, a flavour enhancer, it should enhance the flavours I would already use if I could be bothered.

Don't get me wrong I'm also well lazy but do like nice food, but what's the point if you can't taste it.

If it tastes of, well just more of the same, that would work for me.

I hope it does or its back to killing and eating as usual the neighbours again I guess, best get the knives sharpened.

Anyway the upshot of it all is MSG isn't that bad, if you can put up with mustard gas you can deal with that shit, so;

Nasi Goreng next week mmmmmmm

Coffee time... and here's why MSG became known as bad for you by the rat scientists research at least my theory the people in charge of the people in charge, paid to spread those rumours.

About MSG as well as other stuff but right now MSG is what I'm talking about, well they knew that it made people happy, because when your food tastes good it makes you happy.

Happy people what's wrong with that? Unhappy people look down at the ground and are more withdrawn because they are unhappy, and miss what is going on around them. Happy people however are looking around often gregarious and notice, not everything, your head would explode if you noticed everything, but just more.

And they don't really want you to be watching them when they are robbing poor people, of all descriptions anyway whatever that was all about too much for the minuscule brain of a poor be-wildered (which means without the wilderness that it so craves) Benderskum

Back to MSG . interesting website

Pharmaloonicals

Greetings to all you readers I'm a rhyming storyteller
If it ever went to print it would never be a best seller
We are not a traditional person and don't have multiple personal-
ities
I'd like to make that point quite clear and be done with all the
formalities

While lying down in hospital full of pharmaceuticals
All my hair fell out and my nails and my cuticles
I wasn't really that surprised with my body so full of poison
My skin was scaled like lizards but I simply couldn't moisten

I'm now allergic to everything, which is a total fucking pain
From certain nuts, to sunshine and acid in the rain
I still take some poison daily of this you may be shocked
Due to side effects of chemo that left my lungs quite blocked

I daily inhale powder straight into my lungs
I also vape my cannabis but that is much more fun
I had a ton of chemo which has left my body quite broken
But my smile sits like the Cheshire cat of this I'm sure I've spoken
There is a thing called chemobrain of which you may have heard
Our brains control our bodies but mine is quite absurd
With taste buds that are almost gone enjoy food I do not
And chocolate burns like chilli and quite a fucking lot

My Endocannabinoid system could help with all of this
But it is often quite deficient due to lack of cannabis
I've seen some clever doctors who know about this stuff
But they are tied to pharma rules so can never do enough

So to really make a difference some things would have to change
That isn't going to happen so why is this not strange?

The pharmaceuticals companies prefer this status quo
We need to have a turnaround prohibition needs to go

We need an honest government to remove these biased laws
That's not the government that we have unfortunately cos
they're corporate fucking whores
Until then I'll break the law a criminal I'll remain
I'll never believe the government because they're criminally in-
sane
Or maybe they're just greedy as they make a lot of cash
Locking away us criminals for cannabis flowers and hash
This infrastructure suits them so prohibition stays
If you really knew the truth of it I think you'd be amazed

I've been a criminal my whole adult life so a criminal I remain
But with my daily cannabis use they say I should be quite insane
They sent me off to hospital to a neurological psychiatrist
Who diagnosed that I'm totally sane but here's the fucking twist
They are all in the thrall of big pharma it's them who pay the bills
So even though I'm as sane as her, she tried to give me pills
If you say you like my poems but grimace at my profanities
Apologies, but they will continue till we end such pharma insan-
ities
So now we wait for prohibition to end and it's been a bit of a while
My body continues to fall to bits
                    And Yet I Fucking Smile

Alexandre Dumas
Author of The Count of Monte Christo
Member of The club de Hashischins
The Club des Hashischins was a Parisian group dedicated to the exploration of drug-induced experiences, notably with hashish. Members included Victor Hugo, Alexandre Dumas, Charles Baudelaire, Gérard de Nerval, and Honoré de Balzac

Not A Hari Krishnan

Arrested for not being a Hari Krishna
So, where to begin? I have no idea of the year as I'm chronologically challenged.
It started on a Wednesday afternoon in Canterbury. I'd gone to Fungus Mungus for some scran. Fungus Mungus was a wicked place for nice vegetarian food, the only bad part was the really uncomfortable mushroom shaped bar stools, much to be avoided.
I cycled there on my new purple mountain bike; I'd only had it a couple of days. My first bike since I was a kid and it had loads of gears, actually that's all I knew about it, I picked it for the colour. The day I bought it I was cycling along and decide to give this gear changing malarkey a buzz, so I clicked the thingummy not really expecting the jolt on the pedals. My feet came off the pedals in my surprise and my right foot somehow managed to get in amongst the front wheel, which sent me flying over the handlebars ending up in the middle of the road with a bicycle on top of me, pissing myself laughing. Much to the chagrin of the car drivers I was holding up
As I said gears were new to me my bike as a kid had no gears, mudguards, front brakes or paint mostly, I paid £4/10/6 or four pounds ten shillings and sixpence or apparently £4.53 according to a then to now currency convert. It did however have cow horns which no self respecting kid actually wanted at that time in history; it may have been about 1972.
Anyway back to Fungus Mungus, or actually not really as I remember arriving there getting a coffee and after that everything is a bit of a blank. Fungus Mungus was renowned as a place drugs were available, if you knew who to ask. Well I knew, lol, why lol? Who knows? I only mention this as it may lend an explanation to what happened next.
The very next thing I was aware of was being roughly woken by a railway ticket guy demanding my ticket. It gets worse.

He was angrily shouting "Billet, billet".

That proper brought me back to reality. How the fuck did I get from a café in Canterbury to a train in France (I presumed) and have no recollection whatsoever of anything that happened between those two moments.

My first thought was time travel and hoped I was in my usual time space continuum thingy. Failing that I guess some sort of hypnotism but then Ray was with me in the train. We were both booted off at the next stop not really a station more of a tiny (about 3 metres) platform and some steps; it didn't even have a place sign if it did it would've probably read

'au milieu de nulle part'

translate : the middle of nowhere

Ray had been with me all along and he said I'd sold my bike in Canterbury for £50 yesterday, even though it was new and cost £200. Apparently I'd decided to get on a ferry to France then head to Amsterdam by train. It was at this point I'd deduced it was neither time travel nor hypnosis nor in fact aliens fucking with my psyche and picking me up there and teleporting me here, wankers. Oh no lost myself there not that.

No I had come to the only actual feasible explanation, I'd obviously been kidnapped.

No that was joke it was drugs, what drugs I had no idea, but I had a few mates who thought it was funny to experiment on me and doctor my drinks and not the first time I had woken up elsewhere after going to Fungus Mungus. So you see that perhaps why I thought of the other alternatives; like perhaps there was a teleportation machine or something, you know proper cosmic bollocks and undoubtedly the result of consuming heroic amounts of illicit substances for a minute or two previously to this point in time, with or without prior knowledge or maybe consent to my consumption.

Anyway I digress and after all that it was drugs and contrary to a very popular misconception it was fun, I had a great time and don't regret a second.

Ray and I started to walk he said I'd made him come because he'd been to Spain so obviously knew the way to Amsterdam.

At this point I should say I'm not only chronologically challenged, but also geographically misplaced and a bit short for my height.

We walked and walked eventually arriving at;

'Dunes sur la Plage'

TRANSLATED: DUNES ON THE BEACH

Using my best French and some of the fifty quid I had in my wallet I Bought some bread and I thought thin sliced cheese I didn't take that much notice.

By the way my best French is;

'Je n'ai pas sifflé monsieur'

TRANSLATED: I DID NOT WHISTLE SIR

Not very useful but absolutely my best French, it was something I remembered from a school play back when I was only a benderskum to be.

We went to the beach sat down opened the food and the cheese turned out to be some meaty thing, I have no idea what sort as I don't eat the stuff, it kinda looked like really thin raw bacon but more beige less pink. Ray said he would eat it, which was fine by me. He didn't though even he said it was disgusting and he loved bacon, cos he's a wrong un.

Anyway I don't like waste so I called over this dog called Shitbag, well that's what I shouted and he came so assumed it was his name. He loved the stuff, he was an obvious stray proper filthy a bit skinny and no collar, went back to shop and bought some proper dog food for him.

He followed me and Ray along the beach into Belgium stopped at a café for coffee nice place with a big garden and a dog bowl.
The owner really liked Shitbag asked if he was mine. I told her no he was a stray and I fed him cos he was hungry so he followed me, she gave him some food her dog had died a few weeks before so she had tins of the yucky smelly brown stuff dogs eat. She offered to look after him that was fine by me as I had arrived there by suspicious circumstances and a very convoluted kismet it was probably the best thing to be fair, as who could have known what happened next.
Off we went saying bye to Shitbag who had already been renamed Hugo I mean, well whatever he was happy.

I'd had enough of walking and exchanged £20 to get a tram. Belgian francs were brilliant as you got hundreds for twenty quid so I felt rich but everything also cost hundreds.
Late that night I decided the best place to sleep was Oostende station, I didn't have a sleeping back but I've always had a big overcoat and in those days it doubled as my blanket, so I curled up and went to sleep. Only to be woken at the crack of dawn by Mussolini prodding me with a long stick shouting something in Belgian, I shouted back fuck off out of my bedroom. He then shouted in understandablish "Get out of my station" and something else that led me to assume he was probably the Oostende Stations version of the fat controller from Thomas videos my kid used to watch.
We left and found a café to drink coffee, before heading into town. Ray did hair wraps for hippy chicks for cash and tarot readings as a chat up line, I called him cosmic ray he didn't totally like it, however he was my vampire at the time not for blood but for most other things, so deserved the title. I didn't really care I'd been working as a tree surgeon and didn't spend loads as money doesn't float my boat and my lifestyle was half tramp, so I had dosh.
I gave loads of cash and clothes and stuff to homeless people pos-

sessions weren't really my thing either.

Oh look blah, blah, blah, blah. I might say more on the subject of money later, I also might not if I forget it's just not an interest of mine.

We ended up in the market square, where Ray started being all cosmic and friendly to people which came over as a bit creepy, but not in a scary sort of way, just creepy.

 I best mention here at that time of my life, I had a thing for red clothes and I was dressed totally in red and I was shaved apart from a small area of thin dreads in a tail at the back.

I'd also discovered our tickets were singles so thought it best to get some cash out of the bank, I knew I still had about £250 still so loads.

However unlike today getting cash from an ATM although fairly common in most countries and although you could get money from them with a UK bank card it wasn't internationally linked like now. Everyone had a PIN number for their bank just about I would think but in those days you also had a Cirrus number if you used your card abroad. I had not intended to be in France or Belgium so I didn't know it. Inside the bank they were most unhelpful so that was useless and I by now only had a fiver left.

There was nothing left for me to do but sit down and scribble near to where Ray was so I could chuckle at his cosmicness, don't get me wrong I'm very open to stuff but not blind to bullshit.

It was sunny and I've always tried not to take life too seriously, so having no cash was no biggy.

Some old ladies little white terrier thing with a tartan coat yapped and Ray made him jump.

He was in the process of chatting up this young hippy girl he'd made a hair wrap for then offered her a free Tarot (will you take me to your bed) reading.

The dog really put him off his stride and the girl soon left. It was sunny and lush and I wrote a little poem;

Poem

Sitting in the Straat
I don't give a fart
Yappy dogs that make one jump
From little girls you want to hump
But not me or so I say
I'm only here on holiday
Another street another land
And it's all so fucking bland
'Nieuwmaarkt' or 'The Strand'
If it's all just this shit, then so am I

That out of my system and down in my little black book later since sadly destroyed but 'c'est la vie'.

So now I'm bored as it really was bland and decided to explain to the two police blokes that had been giving me funny looks, that I'm not a Hari Krishnan no matter what they thought, I had decided it must be my red clothes and they perhaps thought I'd soon be chanting at them.

Lo and behold I soon was, but first I babbled at them for a while about realising what it must look like with my red clothes and strange haircut but I definitely wasn't one.

Then suddenly I was thrust face first into a wall with a machine pistol prodding both sides of my ribcage.

To be fair my whole life at that time was a little bit surreal is about the best way of describing it, so I found it funny and started to giggle. Which urged them to prod harder and shout louder which made it seem more surreal still.

So I started hopping up and down chanting Hari Krishna but first saying If you want me to be a Hari Krishnan that bad here we go. Their faces got more surreal the redder they went.

I continued to chant
Hari Krishna Hari Rama
Krishna Krishna
You're so dumber

 I vaguely heard Ray screaming in the background stop they're gonna shoot you.

I continued to sing

They didn't shoot me of course, or if they did this is like Jacobs ladder and this whole life since has been made up by my imagination in the split seconds before my death, when they pumped me full of lead.

At that point, in the life that I now philosophically, only assume to be real a police car and a police van arrived. An officer jumped out handcuffed me and took me away from the fine gentlemen I had harassed so badly in my claim, which I still uphold today; I'm most definitely not a Hari Krishna follower.

Next thing I'm driven off in the back of the police car. A police man with pips or something on his shoulder actually maybe chips in front with the driver.

I asked him why I'm under arrest he replied that I wasn't, to which I held up my handcuffed hands and went der what the fuck are these then, He apologised and took them off. I then said "can you stop the car then so I can go". He replied "no as I was helping him with his enquiries" To which I replied "well that's nice of me isn't it"

 "How am I helping" I asked.

"You seem to fit the description of one of the people we are looking for" was his answer

His answer was a classic, well maybe not but it was starting to get bizarre again

"OK" I said, remember I had no recollection of the night before, so my brain thinks, France, Belgium they both speak French even if its only some of them in Belgium I'm thinking it must be close because I walked here mostly, could be something I did off my tits, oops.

"A bald guy wearing red clothes, then?" I said.

"No" he replied

"So what did he look like" I needless to say asked, but would never have guessed his retort would be

"He had long hair and wore black".

"Have you even looked at me at any time , since I started helping with your enquiries" I asked adding "because I'm a bald guy who isn't a Hari Krishnan wearing red"

"You may have cut your hair and changed your clothes, since the burglary" he replied.

"Burglary, what did I nick?" it had now become so totally surreal and I had to find my way reality and fast.

Think fast and bling like a light bulb in my head, I said "Look in my passport at my photo then look at the date not long enough for me to grow long". But wait a second I said "this is the supposed scenario I've burgled somewhere, changed my appearance so as not to be caught, clever. Then uncleverly instead of laying low, annoyed two blue clad buffoons in the market square, which culminated in me being here not under arrest in your car".

Just then we pulled in at a hotel. The scene of the burglary the owner of the hotel an English lady came to the desk and was so angry at the police blokey, for in her words bringing yet another random person for her to pin the blame on without ever really looking for the real burglars, her little yappy dog attacked his ankles. I laughed he looked at me and said "You can go".

I told him I have no idea where I am, to which he replied that I was in the town of Oostende and I'd better have left by this evening or I'd be arrested for vagrancy. So I jumped a train and left never made to Amsterdam that time, although I've spent a few good minutes there since.

Dimethyltryptamine

Transcendental almost mental
Treading paths previously untrodden
Or are they merely just forgotten
Forbidden truths from eye and tooth
Without a single shred of proof
Taking a long hard lingering look
Into my minds inexorable book
I'll huff and I'll puff
but it's all just some stuff
Wherever will it come to an end?
Over here over there or just around the bend
Or perhaps with luck even further yet
But that style of patience is impossible I'd bet
Impossible for the naked mind to behold
Without the need for being bold
But permitting your mind to really unfold
Curling around that wonderful infinitesimal sound
Removing clothing to realign with the ground
Touching the universe being the earth
Wondrous sensation from our place of birth
But it's broken and burned
nature unturned
Is this all it can be and all that we've learned?
From the past we've remembered very little
Hence our lives have become very brittle
Ready to fall back out from this trip
But truly is that really it?

Miranda And The Seven Pillars

For medicinal use cannabis is legal, now that's an unusual stance
Legal or illegal are ridiculous words for plants
What is illegal is human use so that's how they regulate us
Let me divulge so you know what I mean, they are sneaky of that you can trust
Production, Possession and Distribution are illegal or whatever term you choose
Grow, smoke, eat or pass on are other words we could use
To the rest of the world our war is over but that's only propaganda
In Britain we're still likely to hear what is known in America as the Miranda
To watch how quickly things escalate till they are very intense
'You do not have to say anything, but it may harm your defence'
Stop them there and refuse their arrest
As they only intend to feather their nest
As the fines paid are connected to their pensions I've heard so they're lacking integrity
And probably also openness as they ignore transparency
And quite often clearly not being applied is any objectivity
There are seven pillars to public life and those I just mentioned are three
Selflessness, accountability, honesty and leadership are the remaining four
Decide for yourself if any were broken as they try to enforce their bad law
'If you do not mention when questioned something which you later rely on in court'
Is nothing but a form of coercion and is something quite easy to thwart
'Anything you do say may be given in evidence'
Just nod and smile as they can't stand the silence
So the only thing truly black and white is the fur on a zebra or panda

And often the popo don't know the law cos they ignored the latest memoranda
When they give you a warning about what you've done
They refer to cannabis as Schedule one
But that can't be right which is as plain as can be
If they made it legal to be prescribe medicinally
But unless you go private those prescriptions are few
Which of course most of us can't afford to do
Seven hundred a month is what I've been hearing
If they did this at sea it would be called buccaneering
For cannabis to be a schedule one it can't have medicinal properties
So arrests are false just like this law they apply like a postcode lottery
So what can we do, if we march, lobby, protest?
They'll just send in the popo in their bullet proof vests
There is no point in asking of they who don't listen
They only care about money and their empathy is missing
Believe me the government don't give a toss
Except for something personal…financial loss
So this is the thing we all need to decide
To come out of the closet or continue to hide
Ignore their shit laws and be open and free
I've done that for decades there's no buttons on me
Well at least none with holes unlike our laws
The belief of which is like Santa Clause

Cbd And Some Other Stuff

Looking at lots of recent news I've noticed a different trend
Media talking about cannabis like prohibition is going to end
But I also see another side and this is what worries me
A push for synthetic cannabinoids developed in factories
Or maybe a laboratory made in a Petri dish
Something quite abhorrent and smelling worse than fish
They vilify the THC, The Helpful Cannabinoid
And every time I hear it, it gets me quite annoyed
I hear this from many vendors of hemp and CBD
'Our cannabis won't get you high', but that's not the point to me
With THC and the full entourage the difference is clearly massive
Without it your Endocannabinoid system will only be working on passive
My research tells me that CBD blocks CB2's transmitters
So if you exclude THC you are merely counterfeiters
I agree that CBD has a place amongst the full entourage
But ignoring the other cannabinoids is herbal sabotage
So kindly stop your rhetoric it really isn't funny
Or carry on telling your big fat lies and rake in your dirty money
I know not all the vendors are just out to make a buck
But those of you who are doing that, I hope you run out of luck
They'll sell you oil that's only fit to fry a couple of eggs
They're the vendors I'm talking about, they really are the dregs
There are many honest vendors and some I know quite well
And then there spivs who would sell their own kids to make their profits swell
So I hope all you honest vendors will listen to what I just said
Don't say 'Ours Won't Get You High' put that shit to bed
It was invented by clever spin doctors to keep prohibition in place
Then passed to unscrupulous people who would clearly lie to your face
And I know that CBD can be good and some people sell it with

pride
But for those of us with cancer and stuff it would not even touch the sides
But knowledge is spreading and people are waking
I hope all of you people can soon be partaking
With decriminalised cannabis use available to all
The taxes from sales just wouldn't be small
It could save lots of money for our struggling NHS
And bring other revenue in to help all the rest
Billions to help our crumbling economy
Grow Your Own to help everyone's autonomy
With Climate crisis life as we know is very much in peril
The end of society is looming and soon everything will be feral
While governments ignore the facts and the truth
Even when they are shown indisputable proof
Hemp in the fields for food, oil and more
Ending the need for another world war
But how did we come to be in such a stew
Don't look at your history books they lie to you too
The people in charge are a tiny percent
And they are blatantly crooked twisted and bent
They own all the media and keep governments in their pockets
They act like they're aliens who came here in some rockets
OK I realise that's a stretch of the facts
So I'll bid you adieu in my tin foil hat

Killer Drug Turns Doctor To Bat

and all that Palaver

Two puffs on a marijuana cigarette and I turned into a bat flew round the room and into a 200 foot inkwell claimed Dr James Munch, under oath in court. Dr. Munch a Pharmacologist of Temple University, Philadelphia, USA was expert witness for the Federal Bureau of Narcotics and US Government , from 1938 – 1962 stating the effect he had from marijuana.

Well of course it's laughable that anyone could believe such claptrap. Nevertheless his word was heard these now infamous words, crop up every now and again, well in my world at least. I read something years ago and it made me curious as to why Anslinger and his cronies (which I've just looked up and it means friends) hated cannabis so much.

So first of all where does JD Anslinger fit into the equation? Well back in the 1930s, his wife's uncle the Secretary of State to the US Treasury Department Andrew Mellon and a very powerful industrialist with interests/investments as diverse as DuPont and General Motors and not averse to political leverage in favour of his own businesses, appointed him head of the newly formed Federal Bureau of Narcotics. So first look at Mellon's business interests and there is an undeniable link between the myriad uses of Hemp/Cannabis as opposed to coal, lumber and the new upcoming 'fossil' oil based, petroleum, nylon and plastics industries.

Anslinger wasted no time whatsoever in his goal to demolish the Hemp industries.

Now if we just backtrack a little to 1919 a newly re-invented machine called a decorticator had just been patented on 1st July by George W Schlichten which would have revolutionised the stripping of hemp as separating the fibres from the hurds had always been problematic. The first fully operative decorticator went to work in a spinning mill owned by John D Rockefeller, who tried unsuccessfully to buy out the patent.

However investors were needed to market and develop the invention but were in short supply one though Harry Timken the owner of Timken Roller Bearing Company wanted to develop it for both fibre and paper production, and met with Edward W Scripps of Scripps Newspaper Company, who along with William Hearst owned vast areas of Woodlands and Forests which they thought would be severely devalued by the development of alternatives for paper. This is true of most papers as Hemp paper is much stronger than other papers, including rag papers made from cotton and can be recycled up to seven times unlike others usually only three.

However for newspapers hemp paper is far too good a quality due to its cellulose content timber only contains about 30% cellulose whereas hemp can contain up to 85% which gives it strength and durability.

Alongside these industries that hemp was seen as a threat to, there was also the Multinational Pharmaceutical and Petrochemical Conglomerates owned by Lammot Du Pont II that bore his name were using fossil fuels to manufacture fuels and medicines and the recent invention of nylon synthetic fibres. General Motors car manufacturer was another industry the Du Pont family became part of building cars specifically to run on petrol or gasoline as it's called in America.

There is an old joke about Ford automobiles from that time 'Any colour you want as long as it's black', which quite likely originated as an idea for advertising GM Cars as they came in a variety of colours.

As far as these investors were concerned something had to be done to put a metaphorical spanner in the works. So the FBN drafted the Marijuana Tax Act which would put hemp production under the jurisdiction of the Treasury Department.

Between 1935 and 1937 Du Pont persistently lobbied Herman Oliphant, chief counsel to the US Treasury Dept. Mellon Secretary of State to the US Treasury piled pressure on for federal legislation, not only was he Anslinger's uncle in law but also Du Pont's banker and a major shareholder in both Du Pont and Golf Oil and a large coal mining company.

With Hearst vilifying Mexicans and by association marijuana in print for many years and the recent Reefer Madness Campaign apparently made by a church group (although exactly who is uncertain the films were later purchased and added to by notorious exploitation film producer Dwain Esper) the newly revived hemp industries were in for a rough ride.

Of course the sneaky part is the use of the word Marijuana often these days thought of as a racist word, I'll not get into semantics here but will briefly look at the word and how it became known. Most people will have heard of the song "La Cucaracha" which translated literally means "The Cockroach", in the song the cockroach loses one of its legs which makes it difficult to get around the words have changed over the years but many of the changes have highlighted political or social conditions originally included the following words;

La cucaracha, la cucaracha

Ya no puede caminar

Porque no tiene

porque le falta

Marihuana que fumar

Which translated is;

The cockroach, the cockroach

Cannot walk anymore

Because it hasn't

because it lacks

marijuana to smoke

But what has that got to do with Hemp well just after the turn of the 20th Century the President of the United States Theodore Roosevelt declared 150 million acres of land National Forests which meant Hearst was unable to cut down as much as he wanted for newspaper production, even though he owned much of the land mentioned.

Possibly part of the reason for the new land titles were a bit of political rivalry. Roosevelt disliked Hearst's style of yellow journalism as he wanted to read a newspaper full of facts not stories made up to sell papers.

Roosevelt it seems felt Hearst responsible in part for causing the Spanish - American war of 1898 due to the same yellow journalism and its penchant for sensationalism.

Hearst decided to head for Mexico where he also owned vast tracks of land; there he came across Pancho Villa the former bandit and his newly named by the President of Mexico Northern Division.

Pancho Villa revolutionary commander and one of the most prominent figures of the Mexican Revolution is generally one of the first names that comes to mind when the history and literal meaning of "La Cucaracha" is questioned. The revolutionary version was reportedly sung by Villa's troops during battle they managed to secure 800,000 acres of the land mostly forest from William Hearst earmarked for timber and paper production and possibly the catalyst for the Mexican revolution and it's also the adaptation that most notably references cannabis.

Quite possibly where the word marijuana entered the western world at first unnoticed but also a possible origin to the word Roach as the butt of a joint or spliff.

Hearst was renowned for anti Mexican propaganda printed in his many media outlets he also ran anti hemp ads in 20 daily newspapers, 11 Sunday newspapers in 13 cities, which provided huge support to the campaign for the Marijuana Tax Act. It is no coincidence Hearst thought he stood to lose a fortune as hemp production threatened the value of wood pulp.

Once passed the Marijuana Tax Act 1937 due to its bureaucratic, legal and financial barriers made it nearly impossible for farmers to be successful in the hemp industries. Strange that in a time of industrial decline a resource hailed as the new billion dollar crop by popular Mechanics Magazine would be doomed to failure.

Had the greed of the conglomerate of Hearst, DuPont, Mellon, Rockefeller and the racial hatred of Anslinger not won the day back in history it's possible the climate of the world we currently live in may not have undergone such cataclysmic changes.

If you know the facts about Hemp it is not difficult to understand how the prohibition of cannabis would be beneficial to those invested in its rivals.

For just oil production alone, one acre of industrial hemp produces enough seed to make Three Hundred gallons of oil with Three tons of nutritious hemp flour produced from the waste of those same seeds.

Further to this fabrics can be made from the fibres in the stems, which are fire, water and mildew resistant, but also thermodynamic which means clothes made from the fabric are warm in winter and cool in summer. Cotton fabrics are prone to mildew, cotton also requires chemicals in the form of pesticides and herbicides and vast amounts of water when growing.

The centre of the stems or hurds can be made into building materials with timber style boards stronger than oak. Hemp bricks are a carbon sink as unlike conventional bricks they have not been fired and literally absorb carbon from the air making them stronger with age.

There are so many uses for this plant that any government that can't see the potential of this wonder crop is either blind or more likely so heavily invested in its rivals.

This brings us to where we are today apart from mentioning members of our government are heavily involved in a monopoly to grow what they call 'Medicinal Cannabis', although anyone that knows realises that Medicinal, Recreational, Sacramental and Industrial Cannabis/Hemp it is all the same plant as they are all Cannabis Sativa L, the L being Carl Linnaeus who formalised our modern system of taxonomy or classification.

The difference between Hemp and Cannabis is plant husbandry and geographical location, however genetically they are one and the same.

The Prohibitionists

Of the early prohibitionists there's a few that really were the worst
I'll start with a politician a millionaire named William Hearst
He owned some forests to turn into pulp and I've read that he was not a nice fellow

He also owned many newspapers but his journalism was nick-named yellow
Well according to the president whose shortened name was Ted
He bought a paper to read the news but got pages of fiction instead
So he thought of a plan to diminish the man and declared lots of land National parks
Much of this land owned by Hearst, Teddy's bite was as bad as his bark

To his forests in Mexico Hearst sent gangs to cut trees to make pulp for his papers
But he never expected Pancho Villa or his Northern Division's capers
La cucaracha they sang as they marched into battle then they stopped his men cutting the woods
They sang about Marijuana a word none of Hearst's men under-stood
In the newspapers he vilified them called them cutthroats and thieves
Blaming it all on this weed marijuana until everybody believed

From the US Treasury Department, Andrew Mellon, Secretary of State
With ulterior motives joined in with him in order to further the hate
He appointed a racist named Anslinger who was married to his niece

In the Federal Bureau of Narcotics he was head of the new drug police

Who then bought in his own drugs expert a scientist/doctor named Munch
You should hear what this guy had to say he was what I'd call out to lunch
He swore that Marijuana had made him temporarily insane
But what would you expect after being a bat how could he be the same

There were others who joined in this battle with plenty of money to add
They financed the propaganda that made marijuana sound bad
But the reason for them wasn't a drug that they'd nicknamed 'Loco Weed'
It was really about cannabis/hemp and its incredibly useful seed

These guys were invested in oil from the ground, along with that Secretary of State
By the time all the farm owners realised the trick it was then, already too late

The truth of the matter was hidden because of new industry centred on underground oil
Three hundred gallons from an acre of hemp can be made...then still using the spoil

After extracting oil you still get three tons of flour from the husk of the seed
But the oil from the ground was already found and they couldn't see past their own greed

But back to the plant there's still plenty more from the leaves, flowers, stems and the roots
From Salads to textiles, medicine to bricks, Oh and not forgetting

the zoots

There's thousands and thousands of uses but that's not the point of this verse
It's the roots of prohibition and to name and shame the worst
Andrew Mellon, William Hearst and Lammot DuPont the second
Were invested in forests and a force to be reckoned
When slavery ended harvesting hemp was expensive and seen to be on the decline
But a recently patented harvest machine did the job in a fraction of time
The owner of standard oil John D Rockefeller Jnr did insist
To his friends and other investors the machine was quite hit and miss
He had always said alcohol was bad it was something he continued to lobby
But he made gasoline he owned standard oil so it was more than a millionaire's hobby

Mellon and DuPont joined with Rockefeller and invested in oil together
To remove hemp from the equation would seem to be their endeavour
Everyone knew of hemp and that it was cannabis too
But this marijuana was something they didn't and somehow scarily new

So in 1937 they passed a new law The Marijuana Tax Act
So hemp became too costly a crop and that was a statement of fact
Then they soon made it all quite illegal except to own the seed
Although this was all a long time ago prohibition is still about greed

The big book of Knowledge

Cannabis And Hemp

Cannabis with more THC = Cannabis Sativa L
Cannabis with less than 0.3% THC =
non-psychoactive = industrial hemp
But still Cannabis Sativa L

Cannabis can be harvested for Flowers, Seeds, Stalks and Roots.

Cannabis could replace Petroleum, Timber, Cotton, Rapeseed

However Hemp Farming is thwarted due to vested interests
in outdated industries and licences to grow hemp difficult to
obtain

High THC cannabis produces 7X more seed than low THC cannabis (hemp)

Construction materials 1-acre Cannabis (4months) =
4 acres Trees (20+yrs)

Fabric and Clothing 1-acre Cannabis (4months) =
2 acres Cotton (6months)

Fuel and Food 1-acre cannabis provides about 300-gallon seed oil

The waste product of producing Hemp Oil is 3 Tons of Nutritious
Hemp Flour

Whereas Soy, Rape or Sunflower Seeds provide about 100-115
gallons

The waste product from these lesser crops could be composted
but is often burned

Industrial Uses Of Cannabis

The possibilities are endless

Cannabis Sativa L, Cannabis Indica, Cannabis Ruderalis (Hemp),

" *The earliest known woven fabric was apparently of hemp, which began to be worked in the eighth millenium (8,000 - 7,000BC)*"

(The Columbia History of the World, 1981, page 54)

The body of literature (archaeologists, anthropologists, philologists, economists, historians, etc.) is in agreement that, at the very least:

'From more than 1,000 years before the birth of Christ until 1883AD., Cannabis hemp - indeed, Marijuana -- was our planets largest agricultural crop and most important industry for thousands of products and enterprises;producing the overall majority of Earths fibre, fabric, lighting oil, paper, incense and medicines, as well as a primary source of essential food, oil and protein for humans and animals'.

From The Emperor Wears No Clothes by Jack Herer

Fabrics;

Hemp fibres are up to 4 times stronger than cotton, more durable, softer, resistant to mildew.
Furthermore clothes made from hemp can be recycled to make rag paper.

Some fine clothes were traditionally made from hemp fibre, including some of the finest linens.

The well known fabric Denim was originally made in America from hemp,
shipped from France in bales labelled Chenvre de Nim, chenvre being French for hemp eventually shortened to Denim by dock workers in America.

The 'Father of History' Herodotus mentions the Thracians produced the finest cloth from hemp.

Shipping;

Ropes, Sails, Charts and Maps were all traditionally made from hemp.

Oakum was prepared from cannabis fibres taken from rope steeped in tars and pressed. It was an ideal sealant for the hulls of wooden ships. Hemp - Jolly Jack Tar

Hemp plants (Cannabis) grow up to 15 feet tall

Rope was traditionally made from fibres from the upright stems of the plant. It was very strong but it had to be dipped in tar to make the ropes waterproof and needed subsequent re-coating.

Hemp plants do not need a hot climate. Rope makers used hemp from Lincolnshire, Russia and Italy.

Paper;

Most medieval books and bibles were made from cannabis fibres, of much better quality than wood pulp papers and capable of lasting for thousands of years.

Paper money was usually made from hemp as it was far more durable than wood pulp paper.

Hemp paper can be recycled up to 7 times nearly twice that of other papers.

The earliest piece of paper that exists was made from hemp c.100BC. from China.

Canvas;

For both;
Tents ideal for Tarpaulin not only because of it's fire retardent , mildew resistance and partial shower proofing properties but also as a woven cloth it's fibres are Thermo-dynamic meaning it retains warmth in cold but is cooling when it's hot
&
Artwork. The Dutch word 'canvas' is derived from the Latin word 'cannabis'.

Paints;

Varnishes, Adhesives and Glues traditionally had cannabis in their composition'

Floor Coverings;

Historically were often made from cannabis fibres.

Building Materials;

Hemp concrete, fibreboards stronger than plywood and re-usable shuttering for concrete mouldings are just some of the applications traditionally used in the building trade.

In the South of France there is a bridge c.500AD. made from a material traditionally known as Isochanvre described as the process of mineralization of sap and resin.

Terry Waite CBE. World-renowned humanitarian and author had a guest house built using hemp for the walls, floor and ceilings, the hemp was delivered in the form of chippings or shavings, in paper sacks from a French firm named;

Chevonette Habitat, whose owner Mme. France Perier, claimed that the Pyramids were built using the hemp, lime and water recipe she had discovered. This hemp, lime, water mix was cast into panels, it's as flexible as cement but 6 times lighter, making it easier to work with.

It's also stronger, concrete structures start to deteriorate immediately, whereas Hempcrete continues to gain strength because lime absorbs carbon dioxide from the atmosphere as it sets. After construction the hempcrete continues to absorb carbon and continues to get stronger, acting as a very much needed carbon sink.

Interestingly a method very similar to this can also be applied to produce 'Hemp Metal'. The German automobile manufacturer Mercedes have tested the material for car panels. Whereas BMW have been using this method for their dashboards for years.

Henry Ford is known to have used hemp, along with pine fibres, straw and ramie for his famous Model T built to run on hemp biomass fuel. When exhibited the car was powered by a 60 horse power Ford V-8 engine,
the panels could withstand a blow 10 time heavier than a similar car with steel panels before denting, meaning it was safer.
It was also much lighter than a steel car so more fuel efficient.

Lamp and Lubricating oils.
Hemp was cleaner burning than Flax oil.

Soap.
Available today but generally only from specialist suppliers and looked upon as more of a gimmick than a serious product, which is a great pity as it makes luxurious soap. It is becoming more widespread and is likely to continue to do so as a sideline from one of the many newly formed modern hemp industries.

Foodstuff.
The seed itself can be made into porridge, flour, breads or indeed anything that is flour based. The oil was traditionally used as a salad dressing, to make margarine and food supplements, i.e. Omega oil. The leaves are often used as a delicious salad vegetable or to make a soothing infusion. The seed was also pressed into cakes to make animal fodder.
These days it is used to make many foodproducts including a milk substitute containing Omega 3, 6 and 9 oils

Medicine.

Taken either by eating, drinking an infusion, applying a topical oil or ointment and yes... even smoking pure cannabis alleviates the symptoms of many ailments. The application would depend on the ailment and individuals preferences.

Cannabis was for centuries the 2nd most used Folk Medicine in the world against a huge array of ailments, further to this with the attitude towards Medical Cannabis on the change we are likely to see an upsurge of it's use for many more.

Below is a list of ailments that have either traditionally been treated with cannabis and some modern conditions that have shown great promise and often complete from it's use;
AIDS, Alzheimers, Arthritis, Asthma, Cancers including the

shrinking of tumours, Cystic Fibrosis, Dementia, Depression, Emphysema, Epilepsy, Glaucoma, Herpes, High Blood Pressure, Insomnia, Migraines and other headaches, Multiple Schlerosis, Muscular cramping i.e. Period pains, Nausea, Pain (including severe neuropathic pain and chemotherapy related pains, both of which I can personally vouch for it's efficacy), Post Traumatic Stress Syndrome, Schizophrenia (despite the Reefer Madness style publicity the plant received a while back, in a balanced plant, not as is often grown for High Toxicology under the shadow of prohibition), Tourettes Syndrome and just a little one to add on the end to aid in the fight against drug and alcohol addiction.

Cannabis is one of our most versatile and therefore valuable plant resources

Medicine Of The Past

or a Cure for the Future

There has been recently a huge upsurge in research worldwide the following list was prepared a number of years ago and has of course been added to with research worldwide. Research is continuing and eventually we will have a full understanding of this miracle plant;

A short list of ailments, and conditions alleviated by the illegal use of an amazing plant.

AIDS; although the body has no defence sufferers report a feeling of well being and contentment from cannabis use.

Aphrodisiac; whilst the effect on male impotence is not proven Cannabis can greatly assist low libido

Alzheimer's Disease; slows down deterioration and is thought to reduce the risk of developing the disease.

Arthritis; Cannabis can ease the pain and discomfort of swollen, painful and twisted joints.

Asthma; 85% of asthma sufferers can alleviate the symptoms by vaporising cannabis.

Cancerous Tumours; Cannabis can help control and even reduce benign and cancerous tumours plus alleviate the nausea and pain from chemotherapy.

Cystic Fibrosis; Exocrine glands that affect the Pancreas and Intestines, Bronchial and Sweat glands become disrupted. Breathing and eating becomes impaired by Mucus. Cannabis can be used as a local analgesic which can go a long way towards relieving symptoms.

Dementia; Cannabis is believed to delay the onset in elderly sufferers but not recommended for those with cardio-vascular complaints.

Depression; Cannabis has been successfully used to aid people with depression and is less harmful and habit forming than anti-depressant drugs.

Emphysema; Vaporising Cannabis causes an expansion of the bronchi and bronchioles leading to increased oxygenation thus making deteriorated lungs more efficient.

Epilepsy; In as many as 60% of cases there coud be a positive effect with Cannabis leading to a reduction in seizures.

Fibromyalgia; eases increased sensitivity to pain, fatigue (extreme tiredness) and muscle stiffness, difficulty sleeping, problems with mental processes (known as "fibro-fog") and headaches, associated with this disorder.

Glaucoma; In cases where Cannabis treatment has been tested as many as 90% have been successful. It's effect on intraocular pressure is three times that of prescription drugs.

Herpes; although there is no known cure cannabis tinctures kill the herpes virus on contact, reduce both recurrence and blister healing times.

High Blood Pressure; ingesting Cannabis extends the arteries which causes a reduction in pressure.

Insomnia; Cannabis eaten an hour before sleep gives, a better quality sleep than attained with prescription drugs without residual drowsiness or feelings of a hangover.

Migraines; the consumption of Cannabis reverses the convulsive narrowing of arteries but also takes away the feelings of nausea migraine headaches cause.

Multiple Sclerosis; well known to be effective towards reducing the muscular spasms and twitching associated with this disorder, but also aids in attaining feelings of contentment and wellbeing.

Muscular Cramping; ingested or used as a topical balm Cannabis is an exceptional non morphine based anti-spasmodic.

Nausea; relief can often be found from nausea especially useful after chemotherapy and as an appetite enhancer for those with eating disorders.

Pain; Chronic pain is probably the widest medicinal use of Cannabis.

Post Traumatic Stress Disorder; Cannabis has been effectively used to relieve a wide range of psychological symptoms from Depression right through to Anger and Rage.

Schizophrenia; despite reports over the years from 'experts' that Cannabis causes schizophrenia, it is now known that the Cannabinoid CBD (Cannabidiol) inhibits this disorder.
Hybrid cultivars produced by criminal gangs to make more money on the black market containing less and less CBD are widely thought to be a cause, proving once again that **PROHIBITION** is a harmful entity.

Tourette's Syndrome; Cannabis use reduces the compulsion to TICK or to behave/speak in inappropriate ways.

Not only could Cannabis be used as a medicine for our species but also as a medicine for our entire planet.
Hemp grows without the need for pesticides and agrochemicals.

Fossil fuels are literally choking us to Death.

Why Decriminalise?

So here are my thoughts decriminalisation or whatever, bearing in mind I am a born cynic.

First of all we have schizophrenic information/laws or at best a system in place which all makes sense to no-one.

Suspiciously Sativex is Schedule 4 (ii). How can this be as it contains the same apparently dangerous cannabis that is schedule 1, which is Skunk#1, doesn't it?

Who decided the Schedule for this product?

Which brings us to the Medicines and Healthcare products Regulatory Agency, MHRA (sponsored by the Department of Health, AKA the Government) publishing a statement in 2016 starting "We have come to the opinion that products containing cannabidiol (CBD) used for medical purposes are a medicine. Medicinal products must have a product licence (marketing authorisation) before they can be legally sold, etc, etc"; so this is their 'opinion' and from November 2016 products containing CBD will have to gain a licence to be sold as healthcare products, extending prohibition quite effectively, once again nice of our government to help to; extEND OUR PAIN. At present of course CBD products seem to be allowed as novelty foods, but this still seems to be a grey area, which I have no doubt is being scrutinised with regards to more control.

The efficacy of CBD is something to which the general public are becoming increasingly aware of, as are politicians. However alongside this THC is being ignored, hidden away or vilified as the bad cannabinoid. Even though without the action of THC activating the Endocannabinoid system, the full entourage of cannabinoids work less efficiently producing their individual effects unless in combination, the effectiveness of individual cannabinoids such as CBD are diminished.

Oh! Of course unless they've listened to the prohibitionists and in this day and age you would need blinkers and headphones feeding you constant Reefer Madness to not know there is something a bit askew with the Misuse of Drugs Act.

On the Advantages of decriminalising or De-scheduling

1) Removal of illegal purchase/supply; The most obvious advantage at least to those in the medical or pharmaceutical professions, would be that more people could be prescribed Sativex or Epidiolex by GPs or specialists but maybe with luck also something similar to or better than the Dutch Bedrocan which has more cultivars to choose from because they have realised many people who uses cannabis to alleviate symptoms of disorders often build up a tolerance to single cultivars and will therefore need to change cultivars from time to time.

This would only be the beginning of the end of criminal cannabis markets, if recreational and other users could have outlets to buy cannabis such as the Dutch style Coffee Shops or Spanish style private Cannabis Social Clubs and probably medical users too who could still find themselves up against stigmas from NHS, GPs, or specialists who could also refuse to prescribe, or if someone had to choose that route the cost of private prescriptions too prohibitive. I have met many people in the medical professions with opposing views on cannabis, I always talk to them about cannabis and the Endocannabinoid system and sometimes it seems to deafened ears.

2) Product Purity; this has improved even in the present black market under prohibition; due I believe to the quality of research by activists over the last few decades and online campaigns to educate people on the ingredients of contaminated products being sold previously on the black market. However there are

still greedy individuals and criminal organisations who will do anything to make more money, so it is still buyer beware this won't change without taking cannabis off the schedules completely.

The same schedule that the UN admitted during the United Nations General Assembly Special Session (UNGASS) April 2016 was nefariously scheduled in the first place.

3) Diversity; this is obviously important different cultivars are more efficacious for various diseases and conditions. But also for recreational users after all alcohol drinkers wouldn't like to be limited in their choice of alcohol.

4) Research; this is happening worldwide with more and more claims from researchers of effective medical uses of cannabis. In Israel scientists have been conducting clinical trials on cannabis for Epilepsy for many years.

5) Safety and reduction of opioid-related death;

First safety this comes from many directions;

knowledge that the product is what you pay for and not some dangerous alternative i.e. Spice, the same right any consumer has in a legal marketplace
Legal outlets not for instance back alleys
Less chance of fire hazards from illegal grows from dodgy wiring or suchlike.

Then opioid related deaths;

After my bone marrow transplant I was in isolation couldn't get any cannabis my preferred pain relief. I was in agony as my new immune system was attacking all my organs as aliens in their world albeit held back by immuno suppressants it was excruciatingly painful. They dosed me with Morphine as I was screaming in agony.

Half an hour later still no better they gave me Tramadol, still in agony half an hour later some other opiate Co-Codomol I think by which time I'd stopped responding. I was awake but my brain didn't work and the world was mushy, not nice at all. Luckily for me I didn't die or become addicted to opiates as so many do.

6) Alcohol reduction; people will still drink but given a choice to use cannabis instead Coffee shop/cannabis club scenario (which of course isn't even on the table) there would be the possibility of less drinking and the horrendous scenes caused by alcohol i.e. every Saturday in towns across the country.

7) Suicide reduction; I have known many people over the years who were, or unfortunately sometimes could have been helped, with cannabis use.

8) Finance; not really my thing but just looking at all the good being done with some of the revenue from cannabis sales in Colorado for instance, speaks for itself.

9) Rising crime rates; As for statements that crime rates would escalate with greater cannabis availability what utter drivel, prohibition was the mother of organised crime and consequently with a regulated and legal supply of cannabis for everyone the crime rates would fall, because cannabis growers, sellers and users would no longer be criminals and any links to organised crime would be severed.

Anyway apologies for going on so much that my Endocannabinoid system needs topping up to regain the homeostasis it requires and I'd best drink some dyhydrogen monoxide so as not to schrimple or dehydratify any more than at present.

Not only could Cannabis be used as a medicine for our species but also as a medicine for our entire planet.

Hemp grows without the need for pesticides and agrochemicals. Fossil fuels are literally choking us to Death.

Hemp Biomass along with other types of sustainable energy production are imperative.

Textiles that are softer and more durable. Hemp cloth is fire retardant and mildew resistant.

Hemp Building materials don't leach toxins into the earth either during or after production. Furthermore **Hemp Bricks** and **Hemp concrete** act as a carbon sink reducing carbon in the air.

Hemp seeds are more nutritious than Soya and easier to grow. Yet more important Hemp does not impede the bodies calcium intake unlike Soya, essential for growth in children.

Hemp paper can be recycled 7 times unlike most other paper which can only be recycled 3 times.

As a Folk Medicine Cannabis is unpopular mostly from the point of view of Multinational Pharmaceutical Corporations and their lobbyists.

Why is that you might ask;

The answer is simplicity itself, it is so easy to
grow it would hit their profits hard.

No Victim No Crime

There's nothing subliminal, I'm just not a criminal
At least not for grass, it's the law that's an arse
I'm a painter and I've used that stuff for over 40 years,
I'm not fucking crazy, but unlike Van Gogh still have both my ears
Cannabis when I can get it relieves my constant pain,
Without me feeling that I've gone completely insane
It helps with my pain enabling me to paint
But honestly guv a gateway drug? That's something which it ain't
They announced medicinal legality to the general population
But if you know, you know it was bullshit information
But for me it's not just medicine it's my pleasure and so very much more
As a Cantheist I felt 'sort of blessed' each time I was able to score
Now an end to prohibition would be the best cessation
Medical, recreational, spiritual and more, one people under one nation
And the freedom to grow whatever the use a positive culmination

But friends and family of top politicians grow cannabis with no intention of pausing
Whilst most growers still stand to get busted with police still kicking their doors in
They grow acres and acres but deny it to us
Then it shouldn't surprise them that we make such a fuss
Keeping hold of their monopoly is all they really care for
Hiding behind ancient hypocrisy unfortunately our current drug law
So if a law is unworkable and obviously broken
It should be ignored and I'm really not joking

Say No To Bad Laws

As I'm a lifelong gardener and I love to grow my plants
I would also grow my medicine if given half a chance
I could grow my own sacrament for my spiritual needs
I could do lots and lots of things if I grow my seeds
I could grow for myself and grow for my mates
And even have cannabis cake on my plates
But the law says I can't so I'll answer again
When you ask me these questions whilst I grimace in pain

Are you disabled? It's hard to say
Are you in pain? Just everyday
Will it get better? I think it will not
Does anything help? Illegal Pot
So why is it illegal if it helps with your pain?
You could ask my government, but I think they're insane

Although in fact nowadays it's just a tad worse
They are heavily invested chapter and verse
Giving out licenses to family and friends
But they are the lawmakers so it's their law that bends
They make millions in profit from their cannabis monopoly
 So they won't give it up and give me autonomy
They are making a fortune with cannabis prohibition
So challenging that is my focus, my mission

So hear me prohibitionists, in your stuffed leather seats
You are losing this war on my actions so sound your retreat
I declare that your Missuse of Drugs Act is really not fit for purpose
Although you are morally bankrupt you use it just to usurp us

And the way it's enforced is nowhere near fair

Depending on if you live here, here or there

I denounce your bad laws that declare me a criminal

I'm not fucking guilty. How's that for subliminal?

None of my actions will cause any harm

I'm calling an end to your war so disarm

No Victim No Crime is something that's said

Your Laws can Fuck Off let that enter your head

If The Cap Fits

I can't belicve its 2020 and we still haven't got what's required
The right to grow my favourite plant and I'm getting a little tired
I fought the law for way too long but I'm still not backing down
Until it's seen as normal fields of cannabis in the ground
But big corporations are queuing up to steal away that prize
It begins as a trickle turns into a flood of lies and lies and lies
So don't be lulled by their gentle words they only want one thing
The activists as puppets on the end of a very long string
With business calling all the shots protesting will have no power
Then they can do whatever they like which won't help free our
flower

They'll ruin the bud and ruin the hash
The pound signs rolling as they pocket the cash
I would if we lived in a fairer world be willing to compromise
But I'm not giving up my freedom for another bunch of lies

I'm an activist and anarchist so refuse to be a shopkeeper
I'm also not a window dresser and always look much deeper
Now don't get me wrong I don't need to be told
I know they are necessary but first see what unfolds
If you dilute what you do and accept their corporate backing
I'll never apologise when I say the words your integrity is lacking
You may not want to hear this you may just shut it out
And tell me that I'm full of shit and its bullshit that I spout
You may think that compromise is the way to get this done
Don't bother to listen cos you know best but I guarantee you're
wrong
However I'll still continue to fight this war myself
And leave the shop for those who want to fill their corporate shelf
I know that there are many that feel the way I do
I'll stand with them with my head held high you do what you
must do

Some call it weed some call it bud some call it Cannabis
Some say that CBD is best but they just take the piss
Some of us have fought for years while others are just posing
Some of us try to open doors while other doors are closing
So hear me canna warriors who fight for what is right
Don't be fooled by the corporate sham it's gold encrusted shite

The Helpful Cannabinoid

The Endocannabinoid system is a part of every vertebrate
I'll try my best to explain it to you I hope you're willing to wait
It produces endogenous lipid retrograde neurotransmitters
Looking after our lesser systems a bit like babysitters

It has more than two types of receptors but CB1 and CB2
Are the ones that are known of mostly and to which I have a clue
Endo means from within our bodies phyto is from plants
THC could activate the system if the law would give it a chance
The Helpful Cannabinoid is the one
That starts stuff off and gets things done

THC is necessary for our bodies to achieve homeostasis
Without it the system runs but without its solid basis
Anandamide is the Endocannabinoid the same except in name
As THC its mimetic phyto that binds to CB1 in the brain
And also the rest of the nervous system the places we experience
pain

Whereas 2-arachidonoylglycerol, CB2 receptors constrain
CB2 are found in the places pain is normally made
And regulate our immune system and more a very handy trade
The mimetic phyto here seemingly says it Can't Be Done
It blocks the CB2 receptors and now my head is spun

This one you'll no doubt have heard of its known as CBD
But without The Helpful Cannabinoid it ain't no good to me
I'm not trying to say CBD is bad but it's better with the full entou-
rage
But those people who vilify THC commit herbal sabotage

So to summarise this stuff it's safe to say I'd need to be very much
cleverer

But I'm just a simple benderskum and not a university lecturer

And although I understand some of this stuff I'm really not the cleverest bloke
I'll accept that cannabis does me some good when I eat it or just take a toke

Prohibiohazard

When I reminisce on my life I can't help but think
I simply love my cannabis I'm glad that I don't drink
I've always used cannabis and not just a bit
It will make me go crazy is a big pile of shit
A head shrinking doctor declared me quite sane
And agreed that cannabis was good for my brain

It's good for my brain and good for my body
Unlike the pharma shit that's really quite shoddy
There will surely come a time when the people aren't enslaved
Perhaps they'll try to understand how our leadership behaved

Prohibition is my enemy it's never been my friend
If I let it get to me it'll drive me round the bend
I'm out here in the open and still I won't pretend
Prohibition is my enemy it's never been my friend
Our lovely world is broken cannabis could help the mend
Prohibition is the enemy it's never been our friend

300 gallons of oil from a single acre field
Now that's what I call a phenomenal fucking yield
You may well have thunk a think so already you decided
That I'm a foul mouthed nutter or simply just misguided

Or maybe you think this benderskum talks lots of sense
Either way is cool with bit I still won't sit on the fence
My fight will continue until the government relents
For in this broken drug war I hope to make some dents

Cannabis amazes me I'll shout from the roof
It's helping with my hurting and that is just my truth

Prohibition is the enemy it's never our friend

I'm out here in the open and still I won't pretend
I've done all this for years and I'll do it all some more
Blah, blah, blah, blah, blah, blah, blah,
                    I'm sure you know the score

Just Walk On By

I hope that soon my actions will be freed
Although I continue to throw my seed
For the birds to eat or maybe to grow
That's the wonder of nature you just never know
If you do see one growing there's no need to report it
If you do some research you may find you support it

Some use it for medicine some just for pleasure
Some use it spiritually and believe it's a treasure

Its potential is boundless believe me it's true
So don't phone the police it's not hurting you
The council will be called to cut that plant down
Those Horticidal Maniacs just make me frown

If you did a little research then maybe you'd find
It's good for so much and that might change your mind
It's good for the planet, our health and much more
It could save them a fortune on their failed drug war

It costs thousands and thousands to make a drug sting
For only three hours that's fact, it's a thing
Hundreds of police and thousands of hours
But not only drugs, hash or cannabis flowers

Also knives, guns and ammo and all sorts of loot
The organised crime gangs are not afraid to shoot

After just a few hours shots will be heard
And this is the reason the drug war's absurd
With the organised crime gang arrested and gaoled
A new gang moves in and the drug war has failed

Without prohibition there's no need for a sting
Because organised crime would be less of a thing
It all really started with alcohol
But that's freely available as we already know

If you go into town on Saturday night
You'll find many drunk people who just want to fight

In 1920 or round about that time
Prohibition gave birth to organised crime

When they banned all that booze and closed all the bars
The criminals delivered in lorries and cars
It made honest citizens suddenly turn bad
For the want of a thing that they previously had

But criminals are often called entrepreneurs
Soon they had booze sold behind their locked doors
When one place was busted they opened another
Because of organised crime and they were its Mother

They became quite powerful. Really quite feared
The alcohol ban ended but they never disappeared
They were organised now and intended to stay
They could make lots of money with no taxes to pay

So ending this failed war on drugs would at least
Take a chunk of their empire and diminish the beast

Some changes need making all this needs to stop
Don't start at the bottom though, start at the top
There are people in power who profit from crime
So this status quo for them is sublime
They're as bad as the criminals but never do time

With Diogenes' lamp in the darkest of places
They'd be quite invisible if you shone it in their faces

Once more I digress from the subject at hand
So why not grow cannabis in my mother land?

You first need a license? And that is the key
The husband of one of them has a near monopoly

It is no big secret they do what they please
They grow it and harvest then sell it with ease

So then if they can do it with no song and dance
We ought to be able to grow our own plants

But they really don't want us to be so enlightened
The loss of their profit is what gets them frightened

Just Walk on by again

The Horror Of It All

I don't have a very sound body, it's broken and full of disease
Everyone knows I'm an anarchist and I'll never get down on my knees
I protest whenever I'm able I lobby in parliament too
But the problem with that is I'm not a big cat
And our parliament is just like a zoo
The government here is a fucking disgrace
They look down their noses and lie to your face
Smug politicians think it's all funny
I guess when more people die it makes them more money
But their days must be numbered and I hope that that's true
I've been watching the media and I've seen something new
I don't want to argue or get into fights,
I just want what's fair for all Human Rights
There's homeless and poverty and foodbanks and war There's fracking, pollution and just so much more
There's toffee nosed arseholes who sit on plush seats whilst every day people die on our streets
I'm a cannabis activist and have been for years but I look at my world and my eyes fill with tears
So I urge you to think and don't pass on by
Or settle for what is obviously a lie
I just want to paint and do beautiful things
But how can I do that with the horror this brings

The Noose

There are many who don't want decriminalised weed
No puff, puff, pass or growing our seed

They're too deeply rooted in corporate greed
   To allow us to have our actions freed

That beautiful plant with the palmate leaves
With so many uses you wouldn't believe

Whose oil can help make seizures cease
Or at very least seem to vastly decrease

For Homeostasis its nutrition is tops
It should be 'A' listed a 'Number One Crop'

And what is wrong with a chilling smoke
   With these outdated laws it's an unfunny joke

But we'll keep on fighting for everyone's use
Smoke, vape, eat, build, wear or even make juice

I hope all the factions can just call a truce
Prohibition is the enemy bad laws are the noose

The Beach

I try to be engulfed in honesty
So don't lie to me for it's a travesty
That someone like me, lives near the sea
But hates the bloody beach

And it's true when I say, that every single day
In my home I stay, to keep myself away
Nothing could sway me to go and lay
On that awful bloody beach

I couldn't be compared to people who are haired
And it's not because I'm scared or visually impaired
But my nostrils really flared the last time that I stared
At that awful bloody beach

Of this I can assure and don't think I'm a bore
I think it's quite impure and for me there's no allure
I'd like to tell you more but really I'm not sure
Why I hate the bloody beach

Nonsense For The Sake Of It

I met a pretty lady in Amsterdam she was crazy as can be
I knew this from her strange hello of Toedeledoki
I met her near the Rijksmuseum we sat beneath a tree
We chatted for hours and hours as cosy as we could be
Then went to have some coffee in a nearby coffee shop
And listen to some music and smoke a little pot
 At close we walked and laughed and dreamed
Into the night with my onzichtbare vriend

In a Rickshaw sat a bear eating Peach tree root
Watched by a man in a Hobnail suit
He'd eaten it before and really knew the score
But don't be fooled by the man, he'll watch you if he can
He's got the key, he stole it from me
But please don't despair, I really don't care
I'll make it anew and give it to you
It's true that I can because unlike the man
Forever entombed in his Hobnail suit
I'm from an entirely different fruit

Inspired By Melanie

Look what they've done to my plant, Ma
Look what they've done to my plant
Well, it's the only thing I could grow half right
But they told me it was wrong, Ma
Look what they've done to my plant

That plant was good for my brain, Ma
That plant was good for my brain
But they told you all it was and evil drug
And it would make me go insane, Ma
Look what they've done to my plant

Wish I could find a good brief, to show them
Wish I could find a good brief
Because if I could find a real good brief
I'd show they're lying through their teeth, ma
For what they've done to my plant

Ils ont changé ma plante, Ma
Ils ont changé ma plante,
Elle devrait vraiment être dans les champs
Et jamais caché dans le noir, ma
j'adore cultiver mon chanvre

Maybe they'll see that they lied, Ma
Yeah maybe they'll see that they lied
Cause if the people knew they'd been lying for years
They would doubt everything they say, Ma
Look what they've done to my plant

Look what they've done to my plant, Ma
Look what they've done to my plant
Yeah, they made us hide it behind closed doors
Instead of wild and free, Ma
Look what they've done to my plant
Look what they've done to my plant, yeah!

Sung to the tune of;

Look what they've done to my song

Inspired By The Bard

Now is the winter of our discontent
Not I'm sure what Shakespeare meant

But with our psychopath government
Making a mockery of parliament

Surely the people of Britain can see
The damage caused by austerity

If I hadn't been poorly I never would
Have left my home in the middle of the wood

But leave I did to preserve my health
Though I'm still not attracted by the thought of wealth

And I say what I mean no need for stealth
I'm not the type to remain on the shelf

So here I am for all to see
Not giving a fuck if you disagree

The world is in danger from thieves at the top
Of societies gates and we are the crop

This modern feudal system just has to stop

I don't mean revolution cos that's just a swap

One bunch of people in place of another
But still selling off our world our mother
Sister against sister brother against brother

Now

The people of Earth are down on our knees
While the monsters in charge do what they please
The psychopath governments are like a disease

If they don't like our actions they just change the law
They think we are stupid but they're bad to the core

They leave the vulnerable to die on their own
While powerless monarchs on golden thrones
Allow them autonomy but they're bad to the bone
It makes me so angry and I'm not alone

When the world is run by faceless people old and grey
And they don't allow freedom so there's nothing to say
It's time for a change let it soon be the day

There's only one world for all of humanity
Whilst they still act as if there's a planet B
I used to believe we had democracy
But now it's obvious it's just hypocrisy

Our world is in crisis it couldn't be worse
We have to do something that's chapter and verse

We cannot afford this system of use, use, use
Because if we continue we can only lose
I never agreed to live like a serf
And neither did you for what it's worth
There are things we can do to make it get better
But that's not a petition or an overlooked letter

I hear people say I can't make a change
An attitude I've always thought very strange

'I'm only one person I can't do it alone,
So I'll sit and stare at my mobile phone'
So get up and do it don't sit and moan
The time is now the seeds have been sown
Before it's too late and the chance has been blown

You may think that it cannot done
But the battle is now and it has to be won

Stop buying shit that you simply don't need
Get out in the garden and plant some seed

We are all to blame there is no acquittal
Start right away little by little

Inch by inch it's a cinch
Yard by yard it's bloody hard

There are over 6 billion in the human race
So let's not trip over let's tie that lace

And soon enough I'm sure that we'll see
There's still a world left for you and for me

Smile

I realise it all seems quite grim right now and looks to be getting worse
How did our people give us what seems like more years of tightening our purse?
And I'm not really sure how I got this drawn in
As an anarchist I usually ignore all that spin

But chin up folks what happened is done I guess we should batten the hatches
When society is failing mistrust gets built up with an infrastructure made out of patches

So try not to worry although you may due to recently unbalanced thingummy
This may be the end but that's also the start and so on but so surreptitiously

Nothing is forever or guaranteed really but birth and life and death
So try to be happy and smile in its face till it takes its very last breath

If you aren't royal stock or at least upper crust
As far as they're concerned you can all just eat dust

If you've managed to get this far into this drone
Even though I continue in this monotonous tone
What I'm trying to tell you is just not a moan
I forgot I wasn't actually talking to String
My imaginary friend…Now there's a thing

As I said just before it's really quite grim so there's only one way it can go

So look up look around and get rid of the frown try to smile you
may not feel so low
I've had chemo galore and bone marrow transplant that's just in
case you dint know
I really meant didn't cos the other sort is a hollow and the after
effect of a blow

So here I am telling you the same sort of stuff as most of those
witchy girls tell
Beware of my locks or my tickety tocks they could maybe put you
under my spell
But this nonsense I spout always keeps me amused
And if you don't get my drift you'll just be confused

But I drift from the point if you know what it was if you didn't
well neither did I
But it got you distracted and listening to nonsense and maybe a
smile in your eye

So take hope from it all as it isn't all bad
And I realise you may feel you've all just been had
I'm just the same I got drawn into this game and those who to
blame
Are politically insane and not worth my breath to utter their
names

So try to keep smiling and take heart from my words
Or dismiss what I say and just think I'm absurd
If you do then I'll think that you just never heard

That adversity is just a calamitous event
So then smile at it all because that's what I meant
As division of all of us is there final intent
Democracy is crooked and broken and bent

So a new ideology is clearly what's needed
Get rid of your anger or they have succeeded

Instead fill your heart with love for this earth
The place where you live this land of our birth

And I'm not meaning country when I speak of this land
It's the big wider world and it's really quite grand
The world that's in peril that needs a strong hand
So please stop the squabbling and just make a stand

Please stop all the hatred it's really quite vile
You're my brothers and sisters and I urge you to smile

It's sad the hate that I am seeing
This from another...human...being

Things seem quite grim but they have for a while
My health's not improving...and yet I still smile

Sunflower Buckets

or Wibbly Wobbly Scribble

Remember, remember the 5th of November
Secrets and Lies Agenda, agenda
Kindly then return to sender
Once upon a time I lived in a bender

Mind and body wibbly wobbly
Too shaky, shaky for my favourite hobby

On certain days my vision is dimming
Probably due to my treacle swimming

I expect I'll blame it on Chemobrain
But no telling the clevers cos they'll say I'm insane
Not to worry cos scribble is scribble
Never steered so never dirigible

It began at the start and finished at the end
With some luck I'm not round the bend

So with paint and pallet
Maybe chisel and mallet
Or perhaps paper and glue
Whatever it is you like to do
If you're just not crafty it's also fine
With pen and paper putting words on line

Stay, go, leave or remain
I bet you can't tell if I'm mad or sane?

Now while I wait for my paint to dry
Next it's the grass that was the sky

When the lines were a pain I almost said Fuck it
Why did I paint a sunflowers bucket?

Sunflowers fill everybody with cheer
Not like Van Gogh as I still have my ear

        Je n'aime pas attendre un peu

        regarde moi et regardé vous

The Pantry Of Doom

The pantry of doom
The harbour of gloom

Alone in the dark and it feels like your tomb
Death is inevitable and won't come too soon

But then as usual it's gonna be late
Move over death you have to wait

But that's not really a thing that you ought to hate
And certainly not a subject that you need to debate

So another day another dollar
So you scream so you holler

How can you be living in this unbearable squalor?
Waiting for the man to come and feel your collar

He'd take you in, lock you away
So you wouldn't have to kneel and pray

At least not until another lonely darkened day
But then again it suddenly might just all go away

The Railway Hotel, Southend On Sea

Vegan Pizza in an Essex pub
Lovely Scran rub a dub, dub
Rub a dub reggae 'Know Your Roots'
But the law of the land means none of those zoots

But one day soon, you never know
Though for now it's illegal so it just don't show

Chay running around taking the pics
Using 'Gaffa' the tape flags to fix

Owen, Rachel, Paul and me
Orange juice and pizza plenty for tea

I tried to decipher all the legalese
But that stuffs corrupt seems complicated to me

But I made a good contact to help me with this
He proper knows this stuff so his input is bliss

Cakes and stuff passing around
Wonderful people amazing sounds
Everyone chilling no sign of grief
Canna Famial it beggars belief

I bought someone a cake he couldn't believe his eyes
Luckily he didn't suss my undercover disguise

But then what I needed was a proper cup of tea
Black and sweet, and then it appeared in front of me

Diversity of folks some old, some new
Some a tad coked up but none were sniffing glue

Thumping reggae and the odd drum or two
Some people looking for something to do

One way street parked back to front
Who parked that there what a silly

                               ...way to park

Sitting in amongst it all writing in my book
Every now and then I gets very suspicious looks
Some think I'm writing poetry but I assure I am not
Just a load of words that rhyme on account of all that pot

Then going to the bog the door I could not find
A bloke appeared from nowhere I asked if he'd be so kind
To tell me where he came from am I so far out of my mind

So the difference is OH between mushies and DMT
If you just look at the genetics you will plainly see

A girl takes off her top then sniffs her underarms
Catches sight of me laughing enjoys my grinning charms
Sebastian asleep on a bar stool how cool can that lad be
Totally skilled individual seems proper awesome to me
A very pretty couple were grooving to the tune
The way that they were moving they ought to get a room
But my shift would soon be over in my undercover assignment
Then back to the office in Whitehall for a final draft refinement

Then another barstool sleeper a proper sight to see
Totally amazing balance how can that even be?

A stunning red haired beauty proper made me stare
She may have looked like French resistance but completely un-
aware

Good to see you Conner as she tripped upon your bag

A very wicked chat up line you very nearly had

When the group of aggie bouncers arrive it weren't to have no fun
Time to leave, move along your evenings completely done

So that's the end of this tale I tell
Of a lovely evening in the Railway Hotel

In memory of a free festival

Spiralino

Other Gaps

There are gaps in our democracy that just don't seem to fit
One law is for them and for us some other shit
Does this make the law seem fair not one fuckin bit

I know that I'm a cynic but there gaps in our democracy
I recently read on social media of a cannabis amnesty
But Brighton's finest police force thought quite differently

They smashed down the doors of a café and a shop
Cos this fookin prohibition doesn't seem to stop
There are gaps in our democracy and they start right at the top

I've been a cannabis activist for a minute or two or three
And I'm proper sick and tired of our leaders hypocrisy
But there are gaps in our democracy and it don't seem right to me

70% of the world's legal weed is grown in Norfolk and
Kent
When you realise that this is true you will know that something's
bent
There are gaps in our democracy and it's about time that they
went

There are people in our government who will profit from that
weed
But as an individual it's illegal to grow my seed
Cos there are gaps in our democracy protected by corporate greed

I once stood for parliament that sounds crazy but it's true
And as a lifelong anarchist that's a really odd thing to do
But there are gaps in our democracy and the victims are me and
you

The United fookin Nations said end the war on drugs
But our government are all psychopaths with a gang of blue clad
thugs
There are gaps in our democracy cos they think that we're all
mugs

But why did this all start? And isn't it time to shatter?
Or just leave it as it is so the fat cats just get fatter
There are gaps in our democracy it's as if we do not matter

The people in our government call us proletariat
They live in a different world to us and don't know where we're at
There are gaps in our democracy and I think I smell a rat

The only way I've seen till now was to break their unfair laws
Or keep it all in secrecy hidden behind locked doors
There are gaps in our democracy it's full of fookin flaws

But we've got ourselves a brief to take this all to court
But it cost's a fuckin fortune before the fight is fought
There are gaps in our democracy I'll leave you with that thought

The Broken Ninja Butterfly

Why? Oh why? Can I just not fly?

Thinks the broken ninja butterfly

With his eyes so sad he looks at the sky

Then he looks at his wings and begins to cry

Then accepts his fate with a heavy sigh

He remembers soaring through the air

With his ninja wings and not a care

Oh how he longs to soar and dive

Although he's glad to be alive

He know it will never be the same

And resolves to learn a different game

Jazz Police

Sensible Nonsense

Whatever happed to my wings said the Kentucky fried bird
Very, very quietly but everybody heard
I don't have arms so I don't need sleeves
And I'm not a cup of tea as I don't have leaves

I bet you can imagine if you think real hard
I'm just a stolen tenner from a birthday card
This might just be some words a load of nonsense, Babble
But every single letter here is in your game of scrabble

As I was walking up the stairs eating a plate of frozen soya
I spy with my little eye a painting made by Francisco Goya
It was called Two Old Ones Eating Soup
Painted on the walls before he flew the coop

With the tickless version of a cuckoo clock
Although you listen really hard you will only hear a tock
Face all dusty, springs all rusty whatever happened to that good
old trusty
Lassie won't ever let you down,
So dry your tears you silly little clown

I was thinKing Charles the first
when suddenly from his chest the cuckoo burst

Which only really goes to show
everything inside is nothing that you know

Yo ho, ho and a bottle of rum
this nonsense must end before it has begun

You thought of the cuckoo leaving the nest
or a hoard of stolen gold in a pirate's chest

What was that he said about a bullet proof vest?
 Blah, blah, blah...I forget the rest

A Very Vegan Poem

When you say that you're a vegan you hear disgruntled voices
Because people are somehow scared of your personal lifestyle choices
I only say I'm vegan because that's what I am
And I guess you don't really believe the ingredients of spam
And if you love a bag of those sticky jelly sweets
You can't really believe they're made of lips and bums and feet
When you say that you love all animals but couldn't give up meat
Morally duplicitous behaviour could be something for you to beat
I wouldn't ever dream of suggestion that you should be like me
But tell me that I should eat meat again, get back in the sea
I would never dream of telling you that you shouldn't be eating corpses
It's just, as you seem to like it so much, why not cats and dogs and horses?
If you think that that's offensive I really couldn't care less
If I'm prodding at a guilty conscience and appearing like a pest
Don't bother telling me animals die in order to produce my food
That's a blatant Carnist argument and it's very, fucking rude
They die because the farmers only want to make a buck
As for killing wildlife off in the process they do not give a fuck
The nutritional content of vegan food is a thing most folks won't know
But unlike the food in a Carnists diet it's very easy to grow
It takes 26% of terrestrial land or at least the land not frozen
To cater for the diet the majority of people have chosen
But being a vegan is more than the food and definitely more than a diet
And probably why most vegans want everyone one to know I personally am glad that they're not quiet
It's much more of an ethical viewpoint on the sanctity of life
Whether murdered in a sterile slaughterhouse or a shed with a

rusty old knife
Murder is murder and could never be humane
Although if you really think it is perhaps you are insane
Then the amount of land used to farm the food for the 'edible'
creatures to eat
It's 80% of the planet's farmland and quite a figure to beat
If I had half an acre of land I could grow everything that I need
And I wouldn't kill off any creature because I'm happy to share my
seed

An Old Speech Yet To Be Delivered

For some time now this Benderskum has advocated the notion of cannabis and co-evolution, not a very common concept, but something to be considered.

Little or no proof positive can be gained from what you will read here, but apart from corporate greed little or no reason exists for prohibition, so I feel I'm starting with a fairly solid footing.

Firstly, I need to take you on a journey back through time, to a while before we Homo Sapiens emerged. Our ancestors, Homo Erectus, Homo Habilis and Neanderthal Man migrated, as far as we know out of Africa up into the middle east and central Asia, where incidentally cannabis grew freely. Like all hunter gatherers they would have tried the newly found plant and quite possibly became pleasantly stoned. This action could have kick started their Endocannabinoid system and beginning the long process of evolving into a version of what we are now.

Which may well get remembered by future intelligent species as Homo Consumerus considering the wasteful nature of modern human civilisation.

Anyway about 150,000 years ago, early humans started the domestication of our planet, followed very soon after by the domestication and subsequent farming of cannabis. The utilisation of cannabis by humans had begun, or maybe the utilisation of humanity by cannabis.

Over the millennia cannabis has evolved from that earlier primitive plant and was used throughout our own evolution to modern humanity. That simple early wildly growing intoxicant has altered too. Into, with patience and skill, ever more powerful or stronger cultivars (or strain if you prefer but strain sounds like constipated prohibitionary bullshit to me) till becoming what is commonly these days referred to as Skunk by the media, government and much of the public even though skunk itself is not often about.

As far back as 1938 there were very likely to be extremely strong cultivars as the US Governments own expert on drugs Dr. James Munch tried cannabis and transformed into a bat, shit that must have been very strong cannabis indeed.

Anyway back to pre-history and those early humanoids, who would have likely come across some of the same side effects as modern humans. I mean the more you consume, either by smoking, eating or other ways of ingesting, you either become productive, (oh yes caners can become very productive, depending on the cannabis you utilise and of course your own personal constitution) or veg out, which is also nice.

You may well think that we humans domesticated cannabis but as a Cantheist I believe the opposite, that cannabis in fact domesticated us.

Previous to its discovery all hominids were hunter gatherers and would attack those not in their tribe and quite possibly eat them or at least take them prisoner to use as slaves.

Just imagine early tribes attacking each other with clubs and spears and then look at us today. We may have come a long way from those barbaric times or maybe not as these days we do the same, but dress up in uniforms and use missiles and guns instead of spears and clubs.

We know that around 23,000 years ago many tribes began to settle and farm the land at the dawn of civilisation, it may have been earlier but there are no archeological remains to prove it.

Could it be an accident that cannabis not only provided an intoxicant but also the raw materials for textiles, building blocks, shields, cordage, lamp and cooking oils as well as a most valuable and nutritious food from its seed and so much more, or maybe the universe looking after it's own, I as a Cantheist believe.

It became so enmeshed in human life if you had a time machine and could transport a merchant from three or four centuries ago, they wouldn't believe that their most valuable commodity could have become as suppressed as it is now in our modern enlightened civilisation.

As a medication it became illegal, along with all other herbal medications for the best (or possibly worst) part of 1200 years, banned by the Roman Catholic Church. Yet as a major field crop it still flourished.

The cultivation and use of hemp in the UK proliferated from the Elizabethan era (roughly 1550 AD - 1600 AD) onwards, right up to the mid-nineteenth century. During the reign of Henry VIII, it was compulsory to grow a quarter acre of hemp for every 60 acres under cultivation, landowners were fined for not complying.

It's no accident that after centuries of persecution, which were stepped up in the 20th century to such a degree the ban became almost universal, that cannabis is still with us today. Its as much a part of our evolution as we are with its evolution.

We even have along with all vertebrates our Endocannabinoid System, and as a Cantheist I believe that to be no accident either, but integral to both our physical and spiritual evolution and interconnectedness to the universe.

Fortunately in our modern world the shackles of prohibition are being eroded and hopefully soon worldwide the vilification of this most wondrous and blessed plant will end.

Then once again cannabis can stand tall under the sun, there to feed the hungry, clothe the naked, shelter those in need, alleviate the symptoms of diseases and disorders. Disorders which are often caused by a lack of cannabis (Endocannabinoid Deficiency Syndrome) and so much more.

Then begin the process of healing our beautiful but ailing planet. With luck and sensible policies we won't revert back to the dark days of Prohibition, known to myself as the Abomination

In the UK cannabis is still prohibited but nowadays due as always to corporate greed the very people who have been voted into a position to look after our best interests are merely puppets to their own greed.

So people of Britain and the World it's time to convince our respective governments to end this futile abomination that not only damages our health but also our shared economy and our environment. It is now and never has been OK for our elective representatives to line their own pockets at the expense of their citizens.

Let's all evolve together to create a saner more peaceful world

One Love and Peace

Leave Nothing but Footprints

Take nothing but Pictures

Kill nothing but Time

Rambling Babble Or Bambling Rabble

I went to the Hostipal
They picked me up and dropped me there
And then they left to go elsewhere
I couldn't see, it was a scare
But I was in the best of care
They do their best with what they've got
But with the all the cuts it's not a lot
They're selling it from under our feet
Soon doctors will operate in the street
Does anyone believe they give two fucks
Apart from if it makes Them bucks
I need to stress we're in a mess
I'm hungry but I can't digress
Too shit to woo
Let me give a clue
You can't keep a good dog down
If you think about a purple sort of brown
And you can't keep a bad dog up
If a bad dog is really just a pup
The sort of thing to get me in the mood
Is different types of luscious vegan food
If Pizza soups a thing you never really should
Then you'll know its just an up dog good
If you really wanna know who the bad dogs are
They're ones who're driven around in the big fat fancy car

They may not be the ones you thought would be those fucking dogs
But trust me mate, when I tell you, they're the ones who turn the cogs
They've been around for ever a really long, long time
so familiarity has made you feel that they are fine
But they aren't the good dogs honest guv it's true

They're only out for themselves at the cost of me and you
The time is ripe, to kick them out
Easy to say, easy to Shout
Remove them we must,
for they aren't fussed,
If poor people go bust,
so they start to distrust
making their world soon turn to rust
eventually inevitably of course to dust.
And then it's too late
nothing left on the plate
they've bolted the gate
So that is your fate
Bye bye mate

Early Legalise Poem

Cannabis is schedule one
But if you know, you know that's dumb

Medicinal properties it has none
Well that's if it's really schedule one

Everyone knows that this law sucks
But the government here could give two fucks

They'll make it legal, when they make money
But for those who are ill, this just ain't funny

So we'll descend en masse, to parliament square
And try to make the government care

Give us our meds is all we ask
Is that such a terribly difficult task

But if they don't give us what we need
The rights to our meds and to grow our seed

When it's time to vote, remember this
They'll be at the bottom of our choices list

Intrerspectivation

Weird World

The sky went weird the people feared
but the wind blew hard and then it cleared
The sky turned blue and clear and true
in the aftermath there was much to do

But that leaves nothing for the papers to say
it's just a very ordinary day
It is hard to see beyond the disguise
that they hide behind to make us despise
The bombs are dropped and a country cries

So they don't tell the truth it's always a lie
but because of their actions the children still die
An eye for an eye and tooth for a tooth
more lies the wars are for oil and that's the truth

It's what they do it's up to you
to believe what they say or see right through
Then put them to shame for them it's a game
to make the world appear insane

So remember this and never forget
for the good in us all is not gone yet
While walking through a world of treacle

         you'll meet a lot of sticky people

Marijuana, Cannabis, Pot Or Ganja

blah blah blah

Such squabbling over semantics
Is probably ok for you new romantics
Divisions? Haven't there been enough?
It's Just a word that's petty stuff
If you argue with me over a word
I'll turn away cos I think it's absurd
But carry on your argument as if you haven't heard

Cannabis use isn't legal or even de-criminalised
The plant was never illegal but its users were always despised
Back to what I was saying about arguing over a word
Do you think it's not deliberate that they steer you like a herd

Marijuana isn't racist marijuana's just a word
And if you knew the history you'd also think it absurd
The word only entered English through a man named William Hearst
He was a part of the abomination and one of the very worst
Another a banker the US Treasury Secretary of State
Who wanted Hemp to disappear to make his investments great
He invested into fossil fuels an industry spreading its wings
With fossil oils in everything imagine the wealth that brings

So prohibition wasn't really about people getting high
Marijuana the word was bandied about by a very racist guy
He was married to the niece of the banker now let me tell you why
His main task just prohibition and to get legislation by
If you were obviously downright racist it was quite acceptable see
If you weren't what they call Caucasian you were looked at differently

The man in question was that and more Anslinger was his name
He made sure the word marijuana would enter the halls of fame

He fooled the people in the west that marijuana was a pest
Everyone knew what cannabis was for
Natural medicine and so much more
Cannabis they all agreed
Was a very useful non dangerous weed
He told the world marijuana was bad
Which made greedy people very glad
But he tricked them all by using a word
That most of them had never heard

If you think that's crazy it's gets far worse than that
It turned a guy named Doctor Munch into a fookin bat
They must have paid him a lot of money
To swear it in court cos he'd just look funny
But funny or not people believed
Anslinger was obviously much relieved

There were others too in this plot
about marijuana, weed, cannabis, pot
The owners of DuPont and that guy named William Hearst
The Rockerfellers were also in that gang I call the worst

Because prohibitionists are all the same
Don't trip on semantics don't play their game

So the name marijuana and this is my point
When you vape or eat or light your joint
It's just a word and not worth an arguing
Unless you're a puppet on a very outdated string

But if we stop arguing this war will be done
Or simply continue then it's them who have won

ABOUT THE AUTHOR

Rocky Van De Benderskum

Ex-tramp, Ex-teacher,

Ex-tremely inappropriate

Scribbler of scribbles and writer of well...

blah, blah, blah to be fair

Anarchist Geriactivist

who once stood for parliament

Printed in Great Britain
by Amazon

46368121R00080